W9-AEV-369

Tom Chauncey

A Memoir by
Tom Chauncey
as told to and edited by
Gordon A. Sabine

A publication of the
Arizona State University
Libraries

Wingate College Library

ii

ISBN 0-9611932-8-X

Copyright © 1989 — Arizona Board of Regents
Arizona State University Libraries
Tempe, Arizona 85287

All rights reserved. No part of this publication
may be reproduced or transmitted in any form or
by any means, electronic or mechanical, including
photocopy, recording, or any information storage
or retrieval system, without permission in writing
from the publisher

Published in the United States of America

Printed by Malloy Lithographing, Inc.

Typeset by Ross Typesetting

Book Design by Al Camasto
ASU Publication Design Center

To: Coleen

George

Helen

Karyn

Misdee

Sharon

Tom II

Contents

Foreword

Never in my craziest dreams did I ever think **vii**
I'd write this book.

But a great man named Monsignor Robert J.
Donohoe changed all that for me. I went to a
reception honoring him and his book of memoirs
that the Arizona State University Libraries published.
I listened to what was said and realized how much
Arizona history was being preserved through the
Monsignor's effort. It was only then that I figured
maybe some of my memories might be worth
preserving, too.

There's a lot of emphasis in these pages on
me, more than I intended. The important point, of
course, is how the reminiscences and experiences
help explain the way life went on many years ago in
Phoenix and Arizona and the broadcasting business
and the Arabian horse world.

We have a wonderful state. Life in it has been
so good to me. I owe it and the great people who
live here so much. I hope what follows will help
repay my debt in part.

—Tom Chauncey
January, 1989

A note on procedure:

These memoirs were obtained via the "oral history" method. For almost two dozen sessions of one to three hours each, Tom Chauncey talked and I listened with a tape recorder running. Almost always we started at 7:30 in the morning, the interviews taking place before, during, and after one of Leah's tasty breakfasts. Once we talked at the magnificent 26 Bar Chauncey ranch in Springerville, once at the Manor House, the other times at the North Scottsdale ranch.

Homer Lane, for more than three decades one of Tom Chauncey's closest associates, looked over the manuscript and helped prevent dozens of errors. He also made one comment that rather typifies the whole undertaking: After he'd read a first draft, he said: "You know, you've only scratched the surface."

How true. It'll take a lot more than a few dozen hours really to know this man who is at once so straightforward and uncomplicated, and on the other hand, so multi-faceted with a record of success in a dozen different arenas.

Is an oral "history" really history? No, because one person cannot see the "whole picture" with one set of eyes. But also yes, because that one set can perceive life and lore in a way distinct from anyone else's.

The Arizona State University Libraries are grateful to have this opportunity to publish *Tom Chauncey*. Only private non-appropriated funds went into its production. Special thanks go to Audrey Herring for incalculable help, and to Dean Donald E. Riggs for far-seeing support.

—Gordon A. Sabine
Special Assistant to the Dean
Arizona State University Libraries

Chapter 1

Getting to Phoenix

When Bo and I, my fourteen-year-old brother, got off the freight train after a week coming from Texas, we were way east of Mesa south of here. In those days, it was 1926, the train didn't even come to Phoenix, it went to Maricopa. So we tried to hitchhike the rest of the way, but we were so dirty that nobody would pick us up and give us a ride. We walked from east of Mesa to Phoenix.

I walked by Phoenix Union High School, I'll never forget it. I thought, boy, if I could just get an education. That school was one of the largest single high schools in the country. It was the only high school in the Valley. I think it had 4-5,000 students. Big. Huge campus.

I was thirteen years old, I had six cents in my pocket, and as I walked through town I said to myself, I'll never leave here. I've had enough of this no money. I must stay some place and make friends. This is where I want my roots. And this is where I stayed.

◆

I'm not really sure why I left home. I used to think it was because I was interested in living in a new place, and my brother was in Arizona so I figured I could get a job. But perhaps the real reason was the discipline at home — my Mother would never punish me, just talk to me, but my Father had a quick temper and when he got mad at me, he'd hit me with the first thing he could get his hands on. Not his belt though, he wouldn't take the time to get that off.

I think that's what led Bo and me to just take off to ride the rails from Dallas to Phoenix. He was thirteen months older and also bigger, and he helped me catch on to the bars on the freight cars.

We were honest about it at home, we said we were going to get on a freight train and come out here. I don't think anybody thought we were really going to do it, but we sneaked off, Bo and I. I left a note for my Mother telling her I loved her and not to worry.

Riding the rails was a scary thing for a thirteen-year-old kid. The railroads in those days had "bulls" who were officers and they carried big sticks and they'd hit you on your knuckles if you were hanging on, even when it was moving, they'd knock you off the train. Particularly the Union Pacific. They were terrible. They'd hit you until you'd fall off. Of course you were hiding from them all the time.

Once they threw us off the train, oh maybe thirty of us. Beating us with the sticks and all. They rounded us up just like cattle and they put us in a room, maybe eight by ten, just absolutely no doors and windows and locked us in. We were just jammed like sardines. If you had to go to the bathroom, you couldn't. They just wanted to teach us not to ride that train anymore.

The man said, we'll let you out in the morning after the trains are gone so you can't get back on. The highway is twenty-seven miles over that mountain. You better take plenty of water because you're not going to get on any trains here. And there was no road.

Somehow during the night, they got the door open and there was a huge black man, I don't know his name, a huge, black man. And he had been kind of watching after me and my brother. He said, now you kids stay with me. Follow me. Don't say nothing, just follow me. So we said, yes sir. He said, I'll take care of you. So when the other guys started over the mountain, he took us behind this building near the track, up a ways, and there was this incline, it was pretty steep.

He said, when the trains stop here for water, they can't get going that fast. If you're ready, we can get on one. We'll get you out of here; otherwise, you've got a long walk and if that bull catches you, you're going to be in trouble. But you can get on the next train when it goes through here. And I'll help you.

And that's what we did. The train came through, stopped for water sure enough, chug chug chug, and we grabbed it and got on. Well, we got as far as riding the blinds, that means you're hanging on to the outside. You couldn't get in anyplace. Five or six hours, we damn near froze. I was scared to death; so was my brother, but he was stronger and bigger than I was. If it wasn't for this black man, God knows where I would have been. Never knew his name, never knew anything about him. We were just two kids and he took care of us.

The only sort of good thing about the train trip was the jungle. They call it a jungle but it's really a bunch of men that have no place to go and no place to live. They're like street people. The one we got in was better because there were only maybe eight or ten fellows. And they kind of looked after us.

3

Believe it or not, there was never any sexual harassment. Those older men protected us like we were their children. I don't know what it would be like today, but then, nobody touched us. Nobody came near us.

The stories those guys would tell were fantastic. They were just unbelievable. For instance, one guy couldn't get on a train going east. He tried for two days, he laid in this hobo jungle.

Then he said, here's one coming the other way. I'll take that one.

And the other guy said, you crazy? Why do you want to go that way?

And he said, doesn't matter where I'm going, just so I'm going.

He went back where he came from. Just so he was going. That's all he'd done all his life was live in the hobo jungles and ride the trains. It didn't matter. The weather's just as good back there as it is up here. And he went back the other way. Two days, that was long enough to wait.

I learned a lot from the jungle. They had a code. They didn't steal. They didn't do drugs. If a guy drank, they wouldn't let him be part of their group. They would work if they could get a job. They'd mark a house if people were good, they'd mark it so the next hobo knew that he could get something to eat there. The mark went on the corner of the house. You could see it: here's a soft touch, here's a place that will be good to you.

They were awfully good people. Just down on their luck. Didn't talk about family. Didn't seem to be on the run from the law. And they really didn't care which way they went.

◆

My Mother got married when she was sixteen. My Father was a traveling salesman, he went all over the United States and Alaska and we didn't see much of him. She worked hard raising eight of us, five boys, three girls.

4   We lived a lot of places. Whenever you'd go to a new school they'd test you, and I skipped three grades that way. Finally finished the eighth grade in Los Angeles. My Father built a couple of fast food restaurants there, then left on business and all of us kids worked there.

We had a little shack like a wood top, it wasn't even a building. My Mother fried chicken out there and sold chicken dinners Saturdays and Sundays. Across the street there was another lady who was selling berries, her name was Mrs. Knott. The corner of Whittier Boulevard and Parsons Boulevard. A lovely lady and she and my Mother became very dear friends. She said to my Mother, I think that chicken is a good idea. People would drive out on Sundays, you know. She said, how do you do it? And my Mother showed her. She was a delightful woman. She and my Mother kept in touch for many years.

That was the start of Knott's Berry Farm. All it was was a little stand, it wasn't even a building. Neither was our place across the road. Mrs. Knott was very bright, very frugal and obviously saved her money and invested it in other things.

◆

My Father was extremely wealthy two or three times and he blew it all. Too generous. He was very kind and very generous. I've seen him take whole families, groups of people and take them in and feed everybody. Took care of a lot of people. But he didn't remember to save any for himself. Foolish thing. He could make it but he couldn't keep it.

We never went hungry at home though. My Mother always had something. May not have been the fanciest in the world but we always had food. She would preserve and put stuff up. We always had enough to eat.

My Father developed cataracts and couldn't drive. That was the reason my brother George didn't finish school. Took him out of school in the fourth grade, traveled with my Father. He started driving him when he was ten and drove him for years. And he was an excellent driver.

◆

After we moved back to Dallas, I worked as a page at Neiman-Marcus making seven dollars a week. You worked six days a week. It was a fine store, but I really wasn't learning anything. I wore a little hat and I was running around. I was only twelve or thirteen at the time.

I don't know whether I got into a fight with a kid or something but I left the store. I don't remember whether I was fired, I never went back to find out. We sure dirtied the hell out of the two uniforms we were wearing.

In those days, Neiman-Marcus was a very lovely, fine store. Mr. Marcus was a lovely old gentleman who stood at the door. When the store opened and closed, he greeted and thanked every customer that came in and out of that building. And he was very nice to the kids.

But I just didn't think I was going to get any place there. I knew I didn't want to run around a department store the rest of my life with brass buttons and a cap. People kidded the hell out of a kid like that — isn't he cute or isn't he this or that — or else made some wisecracks. Philip Morris — it was that kind of a suit with the little pillbox hat.

In school I had been a poor grammar student, wasn't much on literary studies. But I had learned to read before first grade so I could read the newspaper. I loved the way people wrote things in papers. And I still read the papers every day, every headline on every page, then whatever stories interest me.

To get through eight grades I went to at least six different schools. Our eight kids were born in Texas, Oregon, California, Kansas City, Indiana, California again and then Texas again. I

5

lived in Chicago once, too, in 1919, when the war ended and they had the flu panic. My Father wanted us kids out of there so he moved us to Indiana on a farm. He was raised on a farm in Georgia. Nobody got sick that I know of.

◆

At that time, the Adams Hotel was the most important place in Phoenix. My brother Dee was assistant manager, and it was because of him I'd come to Arizona. I was supposed to be eighteen to work there, but hell everyone knew I wasn't — I really was only thirteen — but he hired me anyway to be a pageboy. I was small, quite small, and I had a little hat and a red uniform with brass buttons, and I loved it. And people were good to me. Pretty soon I was making $100 in tips some days, and sometimes, even more than that.

All the money I was getting as a pageboy I'd blow every day. Just like any idiot kid. Tips and food. I went nuts. I'd give money to kids. I'd tip the waitress five dollars. Stupid, stupid things. How does a thirteen-year-old kid have any sense when he goes from poverty, riding a freight train to Phoenix, and ends up making $100 a day? I had no sense at all about money. No values. I bought a Packard car as long as this building which I immediately drove to California and left on the desert. I blew it up. It was an old junker, but it looked pretty good to a kid. Very illegal. In those days you didn't have to have a driver's license. Nobody paid attention to it.

The Adams in Phoenix was like the Statue of Liberty is to the U.S. This is where all the people gathered. It was where everything happened and you knew everybody. It was a melting pot. It was the place everybody came to get to know everybody. The Senate and the House, they all stayed there. The copper companies came to stay there, everybody that came to town. The chiefs of the tribes, they were all there. The governors, anybody who had anything to do with Arizona came and stayed at the Adams Hotel.

Now remember, the Westward Ho was not yet built. The Professional Building was not built. The Security Building was not built. The Biltmore was not built. Camelback Inn was not built. It was desert. It was a little town in the middle of the desert of less than 30,000 people.

At the Adams Hotel, that's where all the laws were passed. And that's where John Duncan sometimes came.

John Duncan was the head of the liquor department. And most of the bills, the laws, were passed in the Adams Hotel and later just made legal by a vote in the Capitol. They had poker games, they had parties, but it was so bad after 1932, so brazen. John Duncan would come in with guns on his shoulders and his troops and bring in cases of whiskey in the lobby of the Adams Hotel and leave it for the legislators. Just bring it in and they'd stick it in their boxes. Duncan was the superintendent of the liquor control. He was the liquor czar. Every time they'd run low on liquor, the legislators would put in a bill to add a tax to whiskey or something like that, so the liquor guys would give it to Mr. Duncan's people and they would deliver it, broad daylight, right to the Adams Hotel, and nobody ever said a word. Year after year. And the bill, of course, wouldn't pass, never was intended to.

On the whole, though, the legislators were good men. We had living there every lobbyist you can think of. The president of Phelps-Dodge would be there during the session. Magma Copper. They were all there. And they did have a conscience about taxation. They were self-serving to some extent, but they also cared about the state, which surprised me. Later, when I had my own store in the hotel, and was in the Chamber of Commerce, we used to kid them — we would have copper collars made with a chain on them and present them to our friends that were always lobbying for the copper bills. Or we'd give an electric bulb with a battery to the guys lobbying for the utilities, that sort of stuff. The Salt River Project. They all had lobbyists.

Whiskey was available at the hotel, but as a pageboy I never was involved in delivering it. I remember my bell captain, my boss, Jack Kane, who was the manager of the hotel later, he said, listen you little son of a bitch, I'm going to tell you something. If I ever catch you picking up a bottle of whiskey, you're fired. Not only that, I'll beat you over the head.

7

There was a lot of money involved in whiskey. I think they got six dollars a pint for it. They put labels on it and called it Juarez Bourbon. Old Juarez Bourbon. Shucks, it came from Glendale out on a farm someplace. But most of the bellboys sold it. One or two of them were religious and didn't, but boy, they never let me near it. The people at the hotel, the customers, would never ask me for it. They'd ask me to send a bellboy up. I never even tried to get into it. I didn't need to, I made too much money in just tips.

Chapter 2

Into the Jewelry Business

Carl Hayden was Senator when I was pageboy at the Adams Hotel. One day he stopped at the bench in the lobby where I sat and said, what are you going to make of yourself? Why don't you go to school? How much education have you had?

And I said, I finished the eighth grade.

He said, well, you better go to school, and I said, I don't want to go to school.

And he said, you better go to school or learn a trade or learn a business and be an apprentice. If you stay here at the Adams Hotel, these people like you, everybody likes you, you're a kid, people like kids. But some day you might be assistant manager, you might be a clerk, but that's as far as you're going in life. And that would be a pity because I think you have potential.

And I said, well, it's hard but I'll think about it.

He said, you know you're never going to amount to anything, Tom.

And I said, Senator, you know how much I made today?

He said, no, I don't have the slightest idea but it wouldn't be very much.

I said, $100 and then some.

And he said, today? Why, that's more than I make.

I said, tips are very good in a hotel. I'll admit, I'm a pageboy and I'm a kid and I'm going to grow up some day and the tips won't be as generous, but for now I'm doing very well for a kid that came here on a freight train not that long ago.

He said, well, I'm telling you, you need an education. You need a trade, or you need to improve yourself.

So I thought about it for a while. You know, Senator Hayden, he's a wise man, a good man, and obviously he likes me. He said, what do you like?

I said, I love jewelry. I'm crazy about jewelry. I've always been attracted to jewelry.

He said, why don't you get a job in a jewelry store?

I said, it might be an idea.

◆

From a child, I've always loved pretty jewelry. Still do. I didn't have any but my Mama had a few old pieces. Every time I'd see a piece of jewelry I'd go look at it and ask people to let me see it. I loved jewelry because it was just pretty. I still do. I always liked it. I was always looking at it. I guess it was because of the shine. I love pretty things. Jewelry to me was lovely. Diamonds, rubies and sapphires and emeralds.

I went down to the corner of Center and Washington Streets and there was a store down there, three stores, Rosenzweig had a store, Ben Funk had a store, Funk's Jewelry, and Friedman Jewelers.

One was on one corner and one was on the street. They were in a very short radius of each other. It was the real heart of Phoenix, and the real heart of Arizona, indeed.

And I walked into Ben Funk's and I said, I'm looking for a job.

Do you know anything about jewelry?

No sir. But I'd like to learn and I'd like a job where I could learn the trade. To learn jewelry and I love it and I think I could.

He said, come and see me again in a few days.

Then I walked over to the corner to Mr. Friedman's, which is now the Patriots Park.

And I said, Mr. Friedman, I want a job.

You want a job? You're not big enough for a job.

Yes sir, I am big enough for a job and I want a job. And I'd like to work for you.

Why would you work for me?

10

Into the Jewelry Business

I think I can learn something from you.

He was an elderly man. He'd come from the borders of the Soviet, a refugee, came to Arizona on a stretcher, sick, and built a fine jewelry store, a good business on the corner of Center and Washington Street.

He said, you honest? What do you do for a living?

I'm a pageboy.

You never give change.

Why wouldn't I give change?

Bellboys and pageboys don't give change. (He spoke very broken English.)

And I said, why don't you try me?

He said, how can you work here for ten dollars a week   **11** against what you would make in tips?

Is that all you're going to pay me?

I didn't hire you yet.

But I did go to work there the next Monday morning, and I was there many years.

My first job was cleaning silverware all day long. From one end of the place to the other. Cleaning, cleaning, cleaning. He wouldn't let me do anything else. He watched me like a hawk, and I cleaned silverware for months. Six months. Every day. He wouldn't let me touch anything else. I couldn't open a showcase door.

I think he was trying to see if I'd get discouraged. I cleaned the whole damn store over a period of time.

I'd come to work about seven and stay until we got through, eight, nine, ten, whatever. Six days a week, plus Sundays during Christmas. No overtime. Ten dollars a week.

He really tested me, and he would lay money around. I'd pick up a piece of silverware, there'd be a dollar bill or fifty cents, or twenty-five cents under it. Every once in a while I'd turn around and there'd be a piece of change, or there'd be a dollar on the floor. At first I thought, you know, I've just found something. I finally said to him, you old son of a bitch, let me tell you something. If I'm going to steal something I'm not going to mess around with just a dollar. I said, I'm going to steal something worthwhile. So quit wasting your time running around putting all this money around this place. That's what I told him. He loved it. He was crazy about me. He was like a father to me.

He had two Mexicans working there, a watchmaker by the name of Longinos Espinosa and also Pablo Marino, who was a jeweler, a silversmith, an engraver, both from Mexico. And they would take me home. I never spent a holiday alone. They would take me to their house and of course, the Mexican people are all family-oriented and they'd have tamales and music and they treated me like one of the family. I never wanted. One would say his wife fixed this or that for dinner and they didn't have anything, six or eight kids, but one or the other always brought me something to eat. These two Mexican guys. And they taught me about honesty and integrity and it was fair and the right thing not to cheat.

Mr. Friedman sometimes would get mad and bawl me out but that was nothing serious. He fired me 50,000 times, I guess, because I was smart-assed. I didn't behave myself. For instance, I was supposed to go to the post office to take the packages to the mail and I'd be gone too long. There was an old time coffee shop where I stopped on the way back. Coffee was a nickel, but those ladies in there were nice to me. They'd give me a cup for nothing. I'd go in there and I'd be kidding with them, playing, talking to all these people. A kid, you know.

All of a sudden I'd feel a finger at the back of my neck and this old man would be grabbing me and pulling me off the damn stool down the street with me yelling my head off. He'd be dragging me down the street.

Get to work you little bum!

This was Mr. Friedman, and he'd say you're not sitting here. I'm not paying you to sit in there and talk with those girls drinking coffee. You go to the post office, you come back. No loafing. He'd literally grab me by the collar and drag me. He'd make me mad, I'd be screaming my head off. I screamed all the way back, three-fourths of the block, but he'd drag me in the store. But really he was a dear, kind man, very good to me.

What he taught me was to be honest.

If you're ever going to be anybody, you don't want to say something that you have to remember, he'd say. It has to be the truth. If you say something it should be the truth and

12

you never have to wonder what you said. If you're not honest, you're nobody. But if you're an honest man, no one can take that away from you. They can take your money, they can take your clothes, but they can't take your honesty.

He thought that was important for a young man to know. And he was very strict about it. All the years that he was in business, I think it was fifty years, including his daughters and his son, four children, I'm the only person he ever gave a key to the store, or the combination of the safe. In all those years. But he loved me and he believed in me.

He paid by check Saturday night, but you couldn't do anything with it. You mustn't, he'd tell you, you have to wait until we have money in the bank. That meant I had to hold it until we had some money, sold something. And there were days when there wouldn't be a dollar coming in. You could shoot a cannon down Central Avenue and Washington Street and not hit anyone, it was that deserted. 13

♦

When I went to Friedman's, I didn't have any savings account. I paid my room rent out of my pay, every week. And he fed me most every night. He'd take me home. He'd use as a ruse that I was to drive him home, he was elderly. His wife was a great cook and they lived at 1820 North Central Avenue. I'll remember that address as long as I live. And they fed me a good dinner every night.

They had three daughters and a son that was in business. Blanche, who married Justice Charles Bernstein, who was not yet a lawyer for them when I went to work there. He passed the bar later in 1928 or 1930. Helen, who married a fellow named George Eisner, who was a World War ace from Germany, and a girl named Sylvia. He had three daughters. And his wife's name was Flora. And they treated me like a son, like a member of the family. He'd say — beginning the very first night — I don't like to drive. Will you drive me home?

So I just drove him home, me sixteen years old with this gentleman sitting beside me and him screaming his head off all the way: Learn to drive better!

♦

He was very active in the store. He came in in the morning, cleaned up, brushed up his moustache, looked around at the inventory, had a chew of tobacco and took a short walk. He always wore silk shirts. He was immaculately clean. Always wore white. He looked ancient to me, but he wasn't, of course.

He'd go to breakfast about nine or ten o'clock. There was a place across the street in the old Luhrs Hotel called the Walnut Cafe, and he always brought me back some bread and a piece of meat, every morning. Never failed. He'd go to breakfast. When he'd come back he'd have a little piece of meat and I'd go to the back of the store and I'd eat. He did it very quietly, but he fed me. He was just a lovely man. He had a lot to do with the growth of this area in a quiet way.

14

♦

At the same time I was at Friedman's I got a job with the *Republic* and the *Gazette* — they were separate papers, the *Republican* it was then — to sell papers on the corner because I was there. And I made maybe a dollar or so a week selling newspapers. All I did was stack them. They'd deliver them, and I'd stack them out there, and collect the money. That was at six in the morning and four or five in the afternoon. I was there anyway and I'd stand out there for a while before the store opened and the old man would get mad and drag me into the store and say, you're working for me. But it was good for a buck or two a week.

And then I got an idea that no one had bead stringers. Pearls or crystal beads were very popular in those days but there was no place to get them strung, or knotted, they had knots between them. And I learned to do that in the store, these two Mexican men taught me that. And I knew all the jewelers in town so I got a route. After work I'd go by Funk's and Rosenzweig's and all these places and pick up jobs and I'd take them home and do them at night. I'd pick up a dollar or two a night doing that. Stringing beads.

♦

My Father came out here one time several years later and tried to make me go home. He talked to Mr. Friedman who told me, you don't have to go if you don't want to. I'd been in his jewelry store four or five years and Mr. Friedman had treated me like a son, he was kind to me. So I told my Father, look, I'm happy and I can learn here. This is where I want to stay. He accepted that and went back to Texas. He died in the late thirties.

◆

We were on one corner across the street on Washington, Ben Funk over on the other corner, then Ike Rosenzweig. Ben Funk would go buy a new Cadillac and he'd park it in the loading zone in front of his place. Rosenzweig would see it and he'd go out and buy one and put it in front of his store. Then Funk bought a bigger one than any of them. So they all played cars for years when I was a kid. Sure as hell when one of them showed up with a new big car, the other one would have to have one too.

15

The Rosenzweigs traded diamonds, they did everything. And both the old man and his sons did a great deal to build up Phoenix, to make it a good place to live.

◆

I was a nosy little kid, like most kids, and I found in the safe a paper. It showed a piece of acreage, I think it was 160 or 320 acres in Paradise Valley. Of course there were no roads to Paradise Valley.

I said to Mr. Friedman, what's this?

It's nothing.

Well, it says it's due. Past due. You haven't paid the taxes. It was 100-something dollars.

It's not worth it.

Mr. Friedman, it will be worth it someday.

There's no water there. No water.

Even so, let me find out if it's too late.

It's not worth it. Leave it alone. Don't have the money.

So I said to him, I'm going to find out about it anyway. Land is worth land and I don't care where it is. It's sure worth more than a dollar an acre.

So I took a diamond and went to a Morris Plan guy who later went broke and went to jail. His name was Bill O'Driscoll.

I said, Bill, I want to borrow on this diamond. I wanted $300. I wanted some extra money for the till.

And he said, you know how times are.

Yeah, but you can, this is a carat-and-a-half diamond, I want $300.

I'll give you $160.

That's exactly what the taxes were. So I borrowed it. Went back and told the old man.

He says, I don't know how you did it. But you can't pay the taxes, we need the money for other things.

I said, no, we're going to keep the land first.

Well, to shorten the story a little bit, we kept it and kept it and years later, after he had died, they sold the land, the family, the Mother did. The store went broke and went out of business. It was in business fifty years. Blanche Friedman died, the store closed up.

They sold the land for God knows how much, but that's what they lived on all their life and they're comfortable. It was hundreds of thousands of dollars. And it's now Paradise Valley Country Club. That was the piece he was going to let go for $160. Of course, nobody knew there was going to be water there; nobody had ever dreamed there would be a golf course there.

Then there was a time when Tom Kelland and all them came to me and said, we want you to be a member of a new club we're starting and I said, what is it? And they said, Paradise Valley Country Club. And I said, Oh my God. That's the Friedman land.

Now at age sixteen I didn't know the value of land but I knew that land is certainly worth more than paper or cardboard. It is certainly worth more than plywood, which is a dollar a foot. A dollar an acre, for God's sake, that's two or three cents a foot. It was nothing. Less than two cents a foot. It was cheaper than paper. You just know that it's got to be worth more than that, no matter what. And it was pretty land. But you had to hike out there. It's probably worth $10-20 million now, maybe more, I suppose.

I was just a curious kid. I wasn't that smart. I knew it was worth more than $160. We fought over it, but he loved me enough, he accepted it and we needed the money for a lot of other things, no question about it. But it worked and the family lived on it the rest of their lives.

◆

I said to him once, Mr. Friedman, how do you know diamonds? I want to learn diamonds. He said, put your own money in them. You'll learn them. And he was never more right. Later, the first piece of jewelry I bought for my own store, it scared me to death until I got it sold.

When I first went to work for him, Mr. Friedman was maybe fifty-five. He looked the same to me until the day he died. He was killed in an automobile accident going to Califor- **17** nia. Went off the curve on a road. They didn't have the barriers in those days and it was a narrow road. In those days when you went to Yuma, so many people went to the Mexican side for dinner. And they went down there, I don't know why, and there was a road that came to a sharp turn to the right, he went straight off and it killed him. Crushed his chest.

◆

The Friedman family were highly emotional about that jewelry store. After Mr. Friedman passed away, Blanche came into the store to help and I'd been there a long time; we were very close, of course. The Depression was tough and across the street had come a place that was called Lerner's, which is Lerner's Stores now, but in those days it was a brand new idea, on the corner. And I knew the lady in there, she was a nice gal, and she is now married to Allan Rosenberg. Lerner's came on that corner. When they first decided to remodel it they had good-looking fixtures. The fixtures at Friedman's were older than the hills; they were mahogany but they were big and cumbersome and not very attractive. It was pretty well falling apart, fifty, sixty years old.

So I went over to Lerner's and I said, what are you going to do with those fixtures? Well, she said, sell them. And they had a lot of them. They just stripped that store.

What will you take for them?

$100.

For all of them?

Yes.

You just sold them.

I was a happy kid. I went back and we could take those old junkers out and fix the store up.

Well, sentiment set in and Blanche ran home to Mama and she said, he's going to ruin the store. This and that. So Mrs. Friedman called me and she said, Tom, will you come out here? Blanche is very upset. She's emotional, she's sick. She's fainted. So I said, get them all together. I'll be out there.

So I went out and here they are. And I said, I want you all to stand near the bed because when you faint like you always do when we have one of these meetings, I want you to faint on a bed. I said, I don't want to be picking any of you up from the floor. But I'll tell you now, I'm going to put those fixtures in that store or I'm going to leave.

Well, they all fainted, of course. Literally, they all fell down, screaming and hollering you can't do that. Papa put those there. I said, look. It's a new world; it's a new time. We can make the place better. Well, after days and days of that I finally got the fixtures in the store.

♦

The corner of Central and Adams was really the center of everything. People don't know it but there was a Wall Street in Phoenix right there. And a Gold Alley just south of the store. There was also in back of that a place called Ezra Thayer Assaying and Mining. It was an old store; he had gold mining pans and picks and they were still mining a lot in this country. This was right on South Center. A little electrical shop, then this Thayer Assay.

They'd bring whiskey in the back of the store next to us, they bootlegged out of there. Before 1932 prohibition wasn't enforceable. They'd bring in these bottles of whiskey. The police and the mayor and the sheriff and all of them would come in and have their snort. And one of the guys one day asked, how old is this whiskey? And the other said, nine miles. What do you mean nine miles? It came from Glendale. Nine miles. They'd just made the batch and brought it in.

They had sold liquor out of that place for years. They'd hide it in the electrical box. Those stores had old electrical boxes with knobs on them, they didn't have circuits. If a guy wanted a bottle he'd order it and they'd stick it in there and he'd come by and pick it up and leave the money. Nobody ever bothered them.

Just this side of the whiskey box the Beckers had a slide made out of aluminum or steel, they'd unload the dough and supplies and slide them down this chute to their bakery. After the bakery moved out, I'd slide down that slide and walk around and see what was going on. There was just nothing but dirt walls. The dirt walls had a very interesting thing. They had crypts cut into the dirt wall, and someone told me that's where   **19** people smoked, opium probably. There were a lot of them. Why the walls never caved in, I don't know.

◆

The Indians were there, too, a lot of Indians on weekends. They'd come in with their blankets, their pots and jewelry, sit along the curb on Washington Street and sell their wares. The Hopis didn't do much with their dolls, the Kachinas, but the Navajos particularly and the Zunis did a lot with jewelry. So you had jewelry, rugs, and pottery, and baskets of course.

Hand-woven blankets. They'd line the streets. Sit there and sell them there all day long. Nobody ever bothered them. They did quite well at it. Even in August they'd be wrapped in their own heavy blankets, they'd tell you to keep the heat out.

◆

I thought that air conditioning was going to be a future for Arizona. And I met a fellow named Bill Klinman who was the sheet metal man working on the Westward Ho. He said, you know, if you can find us a place to work, we can get a Franklin car and build an air conditioner. We can build you a cooler that will cool your screen porch off. Well, a Franklin car had a big — it looked like a squirrel cage-blower, only they were about three or four inches wide so you had to use two or three. We put three on an axle to get more air and of course it sung and rattled and raised an awful racket. We put that in a box, put the stuff you use for pads, excelsior, we'd put that in there and then put a little hose and a trough and we'd run water and turn on a fan. The fan made so much damn noise it would run you out, but it cooled the place off.

So we kept messing with those, and then I went to the jewelry store and I talked the old man into letting me build an air conditioner in the store. There were three ovens underneath, Phoenix Bakery, which later became the Holsum Bakery. It was hot. They'd bake all night and we'd come in in the morning, so I talked the old man into letting me build this air conditioning thing. It was a big unit. We finally cooled it to an acceptable level. You could at least live in there.

20   They'd bake pies and bread all night. In those days, they had these round glass things in the sidewalks and of course, some of them had holes in them and they'd put these pies out on sawhorses to cool, and then they'd take them out and deliver them the next day. Of course, the dirt and stuff would trickle through, so a lot of people ate pies with dirt on them, I'm sure. But great food.

◆

I knew only one person in the whole bunch of us kids that ran around together, grew up together, that even tried marijuana. And he would go to Mexico and get it and he would try to tell us about drifting off. The ethereal things about it. But he was the only one. And he ended up in bad shape.

I was thirteen when I had my first drink of alcohol. We made it, me and a bunch of kids. Somebody told us that if you took grapefruit and fermented it you could make alcohol. So we got a crock and decided to try it. It's a wonder it didn't kill us. We made it and it succeeded in making us very sick, but that's about it.

I also first smoked about the same time. That's probably the worst thing I've ever done because I never stopped. I thought I was adult, smart. Stupid. I smoked until I had my open heart surgery.

I didn't go to school but then in those days no one cared whether you went or not. I never saw a truant officer, maybe there wasn't any. I enrolled in some night school classes at Phoenix Union, but I wasn't very good at it.

◆

Earlier, I had learned to drive by doing. There was no other way.

My first car I paid ten dollars for in 1921, when I was eight years old, on La Jolla Boulevard in Pico, California. I paid one dollar a week on it. I tried to fix it, to make it run. I thought when you did the rings that you filed them and I took the car apart and I started filing them. Of course I ruined the rings. I finally got it working after months. The first day the car would run, I went into the house to clean up. My brother took it for a drive and ran into a building with it. First day. So we put it back together and I drove it for a long time. I had to sit up on a piece of wood block to see where I was going.

21

◆

After Friedman's, it was 206 East Washington, Tom Chauncey Jewelers. I had the audacity to open my own jewelry store and I put up a sign, Money to Loan. I didn't have thirty cents. Of course, 206 East Washington is where the Phoenix Symphony now is; some people named Lutfy owned some property down there. He was a blind attorney and his mother's name was Wadiha Lutfy, Syrian family.

And I went to them and I said, I'd like to get some space to start a jewelry store, go in business for myself. I don't have any money but I can pay you the first month's rent.

They said, okay. What are you going to do for showcases?

I said, I'm going to build them. So a friend and I went down to this lumber yard and we built the showcases and put them in there and I opened the store, money to loan, which was stupid. Just a kid.

I did make some small loans. Five dollars. Seven dollars. People were hungry. People were having a rough time. And I couldn't stand it, just couldn't stand it. People with these sad stories, although I made some awfully good friends, it was very tough. People coming in with babies. It was very distasteful and I finally said even if I go broke, I'm not going to do this. I quit it. The pawn and loan business was a good way to get merchandise and it was a very lucrative business. But you were dealing on the terrible conditions of other people. Very distasteful. I got out of it.

Fortunately, I had friends in the jewelry business that I had known as a kid growing up who loaned me consignment merchandise. I filled it up with diamonds and watches. The first big thing I sold was a star sapphire for $300. It's probably worth $20,000 today. Nobody knew what it was. I wasn't sure I knew what it was, but I knew it was something special. It was bought by a gal named Grosso, of Grosso's Confectionery where all the kids hung out. She was the older sister of the family, Lena Grosso. That was the first big money I ever made on a piece of jewelry.

That star sapphire ring, I knew I had something special. Nobody knew what a star sapphire was. And I really sweated until I sold it. I did learn. I learned a lot about star sapphires. It was about three months before it sold.

It wasn't much of a store. It was narrow and maybe only ten or twelve feet wide, thirty feet deep. And we didn't even need that much room. I didn't have that much merchandise.

Then one day John Rockwell and Jack Kane walked into the store. And they said, we'd like you to move home, back to the Adams Hotel.

And I said, home? I can't afford this.

They said, we've got a place, they're moving the barber shop downstairs. We think it will make a good place for a jewelry store and give you a chance.

I said, I don't have any money for that.

You don't need any money. When you start making money you can pay rent. You don't have to have any money. If you need some fixtures or something then we can help you with that.

Well, I have a few dollars but not much.

The place is yours. You better move down there.

That was 1941. Then Pearl Harbor hit, business started booming, it started making money like a slot machine. And Luke Field started to build and you could sell any piece of jewelry you could get a hold of. Then it was a case of getting merchandise to sell, not how good a salesman you were.

Parker Pens, you could sell all of them. You had to hide them when a package came in. But I knew Mr. Parker himself when I was a kid working for the Friedmans. I called him and told him what I was doing and he said, yeah, I'll sell you some merchandise.

I got a lot of merchandise that way from people. The minute things would come in they were gone. Elgin watches. Hamilton watches. They just walked out as fast as you got them in. And business boomed. It became awfully good. In no time I had paid my showcases off. I was paying rent. But long hours. You opened at eight and you were there until ten, six days a week. It was right there in the lobby of the Adams. I lived downstairs in the basement, a sleeping room eight by ten, ten by ten, something like that.

I met an old gentleman by the name of Oscar Hyman, out of New York, who supplied places like Tiffany and Schree's, Van Cleef, the great stores of the country. And he said, we will supply the merchandise to you a couple of times a year and bring it in to you and show you how to get started in the color stones.

It was just another case of an elderly gentleman being nice to me. He had no sons. He had a lot of brothers. And he had a famous old company, it's still there. He helped me get started on the finer pieces of jewelry. And that's really where I learned the color stones and the sapphires. Star sapphires weren't even known in those days. They became known, of course. We even put in a manufacturing department. A brash kid who didn't know any better, I was.

As time went on, the store grew and developed. New lines were added. It became quite a big business. It became quite famous for fine diamonds and rubies and emeralds. There was no one else in town really at that time catering to that kind of customer.

Eventually I got help, especially Billie Sorlie, who just passed away recently. She was with me thirty-some years and after I got so involved with the television station, she really ran the place.

Through the years, I did a lot of appraising work for estates and insurance companies and never charged for it. About the only store in the country that didn't charge. Everyone had to have appraisals for insurance or estate tax purposes. I felt rather than charging the customer we made friends. I had the reputation for honesty and knowledge in precious stones, gold, jewelry and I was accepted. We appraised an awful lot of jewelry. It was not an income producing part of the jewelry business for me. I did it because I liked to do it. It brought customers.

Chapter 3

Growing
with Phoenix

There's a story about the old big league New York Giants
baseball club. When they came to Phoenix for spring training
they stayed at a motel and I remember the owner Horace
Stoneham would come in to the Adams and we all became
friends. One year when the season was over he said, we'd like
to stay at the Adams when we come back next year for spring
training, we can be closer to our people, handle it better. Is
there any chance?

The problem was, that was the cream of the season.
That's when you made your money in a hotel. But John Rockwell
was very civic minded. He was the grandson of J.C. Adams,
son of Margaret Rockwell, who was Margaret Adams, and he
ran the hotel. He said, we'll be glad to take you.

Next year, this was in the early 1950s, it was about time
for spring training and I was in John's office talking about something, and the phone rang and his secretary said, Mr. Stoneham
is calling. He and Jack Kane and I were sitting around, Jack
Kane was the manager of the hotel and I had worked for him
when I was a pageboy and he was bell captain.

Mr. Stoneham said, John, we'd like you to do us a favor.
We have a new guy named Willie Mays, we have several black
people and we don't know where to go. The motel used to get
us some rooms in private homes for them. And we'd like to get
somebody to help us get rooms for the black ball players. John
said, they won't go into any private homes. They'll be here at
the Adams Hotel.

You can take them?

Of course. That's ridiculous. We will not farm them out. They'll stay here like everybody else. They'll be treated the same.

Can they go into the restaurants?

Absolutely. They can go into the restaurants and any place else in the hotel. They'll be guests like anyone else.

Well, that was absolutely the first of its kind. The Adams Hotel was a very conservative area. Good people but also a bunch of really rugged individuals hanging around. You had cowboys, Indians, and really rugged old timers, the heart of Arizona. Roughnecks, rough and tumble guys, you had them all.

The first morning — of course Willie Mays wasn't even known then, he was just a kid, just come up — John Rockwell said, we better all go into the Range, which is what the coffee shop was called, and sit down when Mays and the others go in there so there won't be any trouble. And when we saw them coming we walked in just before them and after them, and took a table and sat at the counters.

Of course there were a couple of nasty remarks. But we just sat there and we visited with them. A couple of people got up and walked out, but that was all there was to it. We sat there and had coffee and just talked about how glad we were to have them in Arizona, what kind of a team they were going to have. We'd been there two or three mornings and we went with them into the barber shop, and one jerk got up and walked out so one of us just took the chair, sat down and had a haircut and shave.

Generally, we said nothing, we were just available. No words. People got to where they were crazy about them, and they loved Willie Mays like any young kid. We had a few snide remarks around town but we didn't care. It was the right thing to do. There were no incidents, no problems. One or two people walked out of the room; that's stupid. They were the losers. It turned out very well and we have John Rockwell to thank for that relationship. A dear, wonderful man.

As for the rest of the community, if you were white, you didn't think there was a problem. But when you were black you knew damn well there was a problem. Very easy for a white to say, you've made great progress. If you're a black and can't go into someplace and eat, you sure as hell aren't going to be very happy. It opened an awful lot of doors, it was the beginning.

◆

Guy Stillman came to me one time, forty-some years ago, and he said, you know the way this place is going to grow, we're going to have a lot of traffic problems. Right now, there is a lot of vacant land, north, south, east and west and he said, I think if we would take McDowell Road, Thomas, Indian School, Osborn, Glendale, Northern, and widen them, get the right-of-way now in perpetuity and set them aside for roads, then when the time comes they need them, then they can just go ahead and not have to evict anyone.

27

So we went to see some people and they laughed at us. They said, you kids don't know what the hell you're talking about. Guy said, I'm telling you someday we're going to be in trouble and we're going to strangle on our own traffic. And right now there's a lot of land out there just for setting it aside for right-of-ways. You don't have to build on it. You can even let people use it.

It was hard to convince them. They just laughed at us. Imagine what that would be worth if they'd have done that. Central Avenue. Seventh Street. Seventh Avenue. In those days, Central Avenue was two lanes and the trees touched. Central Avenue looked like a tunnel. The road was beautiful.

The thing that stood out in Phoenix, of course, in those days, was the Adams Hotel with that extra room over the street. And the only reason they were allowed to build out there, they had to have that for a screen room. The people couldn't stay inside the building, it was too hot. No air conditioning. If you'll look at the hotel there now, they've got an overhang onto the sidewalk, a wide sidewalk. That was there because it was grandfathered in.

When they built the old Adams Hotel after the first one burned, they had to have a screened porch, it was the full length of the hotel and open. People slept out there. You couldn't sleep in the building. At night you walked out the door and then into this dormitory area. It was 250 feet long, with single cots just lined up, no cubicles, no walls, four or five months of the year. You couldn't go in the building. It was miserable.

Guests would put a washtub in their room and fill it with ice and put two sticks up and they'd put towels on them and they'd put a towel down on the ice and then put the fans on that and try to cool the room.

They tried everything. Very few things worked. It was miserably hot. A lot of people would stay in the bathtub. They'd fill the bathtub with cold water and they'd sleep in there at night, as long as they could stand it. But outside was really the only place that you could sleep easily. Nobody got into any trouble.

You'd walk to work, which I had to do, down from McDowell Road south. Everybody was asleep in the front yard. And when they got up they'd put their cots up against the wall. Nobody ever bothered them. Nobody ever got hurt. I never heard of a problem. Everybody slept outside in the yard. They'd wet the cots. They'd have a sheet and they'd wet it for evaporation.

The people who could, left town to get away from the heat, went to Iron Springs, northern Arizona, Prescott, Flagstaff. Santa Monica was full of Phoenicians. La Jolla, San Diego, Long Beach. We were on the choicest corner in Arizona in a jewelry store, but in the summer months there was no business. Everybody left.

There were all kinds of ideas for cooling but nothing worked. They had an ammonia thing that would blow up, and when it did, it would practically kill everybody — or would if they didn't get out of the building. It was a different type of air conditioning. They used ammonia like they use in refrigerated cases. Every cockamamie thing you can think of was tried.

When we first started using evaporative coolers, it probably added five dollars a month cost to a house. Utilities were cheap. That's all you had, too. You could really cool a house for five or ten dollars in those days. But they weren't very big houses and that was evaporative. When refrigeration came along you could do that for twenty-five or thirty dollars. Now it costs a lot of money to run the air.

◆

In those days before air conditioning or even swamp coolers, many of the business leaders would walk to work in downtown Phoenix. I'd see them coming along, especially the bankers, no coat but a long-sleeve shirt open at the neck. They'd be carrying their tie, and when they got inside at the desk, they'd put on the tie.

◆

E. E. Brown owned this place right out here, where my Scottsdale ranch is, he owned all of it including the city of Scottsdale, he and his father, and they called it the Brown Land and Cattle Company. And there were no roads here, of course. It was a cattle ranch. And Brownie lived right out near Pinnacle Peak and came to town maybe once a year, or two years.

Philip Tovrea's father was Ed Tovrea. He came here in the 1800s and built an empire of cattle. His son, Phil Tovrea Sr. had right out on Van Buren Street just a few miles from town a feed lot for 100,000 head of cattle at one time. He had a huge packing plant. He had a fertilizer plant and a large conglomerate of ranches. California, New Mexico, Nevada, Arizona. He was extremely, extremely large in cattle. A real cattle baron. And he was bright and capable and probably knew more about the meat business than anybody. He ran that company for years. He would buy cattle from Mexico as well as from every place else. He had children: Ed, named after his grandfather; Phil, Jr. named after Philip Sr., and Tito or Ellen Tovrea named after her mother.

Ellen Tito Tovrea was interesting. After her children were raised and full grown, she went back and became a doctor. Medical doctor. Ed and Phil went to the service for World War II. Both of them were shot down. Both were in prisoner of war camps for a long time. One of them escaped, I don't know which. It was tough. And during that time I spent an awful lot of time with their father. They came back all in one piece but they obviously had suffered and they wanted to play. They really wanted to play, they wanted to have fun.

The whole family were customers of mine. They never came to buy until Christmas Eve. They never came in the damn store once unless it was Christmas Eve, time to close, and buy their presents. And they always bought beautiful things.

But you could just depend. I was standing there about to close one Christmas Eve and the next I knew, two hands grabbed my arms and put them behind my back and lifted me up.

Let's go have a drink.

You know I don't drink. I don't want to drink.

We said, let's go have a drink.

So they lifted me up off the floor and held my hands and opened a bottle and made me drink.

Oh God, I was sick.

♦

Phil, Sr. and a group of us opened a store called Gene Autry's Western Store, which was at the corner of Central and Adams. Extremely successful. None of us really had time to run it, so we finally closed it up. But after the boys came back from World War II, Phil Tovrea, Sr. sold everything he had. Big ranch. Fantastic packing plant. Cottonseed oil and oil wells. He just sold it all. Went to California, bought him a big yacht and just sat there and enjoyed it. He wanted away. He was broken-hearted about his kid, one was very sick. He loved them dearly and he was a good father. The whole family was rugged. They lived and died in the way they were and they helped build Arizona into one hell of a state. They were so bombastic and so strong and a lot of people had the wrong impression, but I loved them dearly.

♦

Back then, the Valley was really a melting pot of people and that's what made it good because there were a lot of ideas. We had them all. And there were no cliques; nobody gathered together and said, we're Irish, or we're this, or we're that. The community accepted each other on face value.

This is probably the greatest thing about Arizona. It was a young community full of people who came here either for vacation or to learn or to go to school.

In those days, ASU was Tempe Normal. It had one building, that red block building out there and it was strictly a teacher's college. No one ever dreamed it would be any bigger. It wasn't very big, but it had a good reputation for teachers. We referred to it as nine miles from Phoenix.

30

◆

Back in the 1920s and the 1930s and maybe the early 1940s, the visionaries, the people who were thinking down the road and around the corner included the newspaper people, Wes Knorpp and Charlie Stauffer who were partners. There was a fellow named Harlow Akers who owned the *Gazette* at that time before the papers were put together. And a man by the name of Dwight B. Heard, who had the Heard Building across from the old Adams and there were some ranchers that were very, very far-reaching.

There was Boyce Thompson, Thompson Arboretum on the way to Globe. He had the date gardens. You had a fellow by the name of Henry Bonsall who owned what became Goodyear, and Mr. Paul Litchfield, who was president of Goodyear Tire and Rubber Company. He built a farm out there called The Tall Wiwi and he grafted fruit and berries and trees, primarily citrus and dates.

William Wrigley Jr., the original, was a very bright, visionary man. He would come to town and he would bring the Chicago Cubs ball club. Then he would walk downtown two or three times while he was here, he would come in and walk down the streets, there was a small business district, and visit with the people. He wanted to know what was going on. And then he would go out and buy more land. He told everybody, buy all the land you can afford. Buy land. Of course, he bought Catalina Island.

MacArthur Brothers built the Biltmore, and contrary to most opinions, Frank Lloyd Wright did not design it. One of the MacArthur brothers designed it. What Frank Lloyd Wright did do is he designed the block, the thing that made those blocks they found when they remodeled after the fire. That was Frank Lloyd Wright's invention. That was the beginning of cement blocks. But he made them prettier. That was the part he had in the Biltmore. He would say so.

Walter Bimson, who came in the 1930s, probably more than any man that I know had a lot of vision. And Carl Bimson, who's still alive. Carl Bimson is Walter's brother and Carl's close to ninety right now. He still goes to the bank board meetings.

31

He's been with the bank forty or fifty years. Walter was always out in front, but Carl is highly regarded, highly respected. And if I wanted to know something really about the banking business or what to do, I'd go see Carl Bimson.

Walter depended a great deal more on Carl than most people ever realized. Walter Bimson didn't get where he was by not having good people around him. His greatest ability was the people he chose. And Carl is one of them. He's a brilliant man, but very low-key, very quiet. He's still around and he's still very able.

Walter had two sons, Earl and Lloyd. Lloyd died quite young. Lloyd was head of the Arizona Bank.

32   The Arizona Bank was developed as a spin-off, and mostly it was with employee funds of the Valley Bank started by Walter. The federal government told him you can't have that interlocking arrangement, or whatever they called it. You have to get off the board of Arizona Bank and divest yourselves. A lot of that money was in the fund of the employees of the bank.

So Walter came to me and he said, I want you to go on the board of the Arizona Bancorp, which is Arizona Bank, for me. I have to go off of it. And then down the road if you like, I'd like you to come on the Valley board, which I did and where I now am an emeritus member.

◆

When I started making enough money, I built my first house. That was the beginning of Encanto Park.

It was $300 for the lot. Now that was a paved street, rolled curb and gutter, 50' by 150' lot with water and sewer. At new Encanto Park, north 16th. Later the Coliseum was built, the fairgrounds, all that.

There was a man named Herman Carpenter. He would come into the jewelry store and I'd visit with him and he'd say, I'll build you a house. I was going to get married, this was fifty, sixty years ago. And I said, how much will it cost me? And he said, $2,700. And I said, I want two bedrooms, a little kitchen, dinette, living room and a separate garage. Can we build it for that? He said, if you help me we can build it for that. You help me, you hold things for me. A carpenter can work better if somebody holds things for him.

So we built a little two-bedroom stucco house for 2,600 and some dollars. You can't build a damn window for that now. My payments were thirty-some dollars a month. We borrowed the money and I had just about $3,000 in the whole house. I lived in it for eight or ten years and sold it for $9,000.

At that house, I would have a bunch of young British cadets every weekend. Now here were kids who were learning how to fly airplanes out at Luke Field and had never driven an automobile. And they'd come to town and they'd sleep on the floor. We'd feed them breakfast and I'd put them in the car and teach them how to drive. Just go up and down the streets with these kids, and they were flying Spitfires and going into war and had never driven a car. In England they didn't have cars. We did that every weekend for months.

Someone had asked me if I'd take some of these kids to church, I think. They said, these kids have no place to go. Would you take some of them in and I said, sure. We ended up with eight or ten of them at a time in this little bitty house. They were nice young people, some from Scotland, some from England, most of them unfortunately dead the first year of the war. That was a terrible slaughter that they went into.

But they all learned to drive the car. I didn't have enough money for the gasoline, really. We chipped in and bought food and cooked outside, you know, hot dogs. You could feed a lot of people for a buck then.

Luke Field, and Thunderbird One and Thunderbird Two. This was every weekend. They would come and they would learn to drive. It was funny, flying airplanes all over the sky, getting ready to go into combat and had never, ever driven an automobile.

♦

In the early 1940s, a small group of us wanted a place that didn't have any dues that you could just go to and entertain out-of-state visitors. We had an awful lot of these visitors and of course all these fancy big hotels hadn't been built yet and you'd have people like General Eisenhower, all kinds of people like that, and there was really no place to take them privately.

Phil Tovrea, land baron and cattle king out here, Kemper Marley, same thing, myself, Rockwell who owned the Adams Hotel, Jack Kane, the manager, all friends, and we're sitting around. I don't know who said it, let's start a Saddle and Sirloin club. We had a pretty nice group. We just took a small place in the Adams, little bitty bar, a tiny kitchen, and we opened the Saddle and Sirloin Club.

Well, about that time you could have slot machines, and nobody bothered to close the slot machines so we put in four or five. We got so much damn money we didn't know what to do with it and we were throwing dinners all the time. You'd go in there on a given night and you'd see some of the world leaders. Really prominent, nice people. Quiet people wanting a place to eat. One bartender, one cook. That's all. Nothing fancy. Great food.

Some would play gin rummy or whatever. But mostly we'd talk about the cattle business. A lot of cattle ranchers, a number of the cattle ranchers like O.L. McDaniel were very prominent. When we got through we had a pretty nice list of about 100 from all over. It was open from maybe eleven in the morning until whenever the last person left. It was not a late club. We had a lot of meetings and a lot of interests. Ideal place for all of us.

Finally, we accumulated too much money from those damn slot machines and nobody knew what the hell to do with it. We were too cautious with it. We should have given it to some kids. Somebody got a wild idea that they ought to make a fancier club. So they went up to the Westward Ho and John Mills offered them free space. Well, they didn't just move. They bought leather drapes and they spent $200,000. So right away it went broke. It went from an awful lot of money to nothing. It just didn't work. It was the end of it when they took it out of the Adams Hotel. Wrong place, too fancy.

34

Chapter 4

Campaigns and Politics

When you run a political campaign, first you look for a lot of money. If you had any sense you wouldn't run one, but I don't have any sense. Or I didn't have in a couple of them. The only campaigns that I've run were way back. One was for Senator Carl Hayden, who was a dear friend. He had a great deal of influence on my life. And when he ran he wanted me to be the campaign manager. I really didn't know anything about it but I did it for him I think twice. And I ran two for McFarland, one for Senate and one for Governor.

After McFarland was elected Governor, one day I was sitting in my office, just a few blocks from the Capitol. And I heard he was considering appointing a certain person who had been in the campaign, and I'd watched him and this guy always had his hand out. He always wanted something. Wasn't a very savory character in my opinion even though he had worked hard for the Governor in the campaign. And I called and I said, I want to talk to the Governor and he came right on.

I said, Governor, I understand you're appointing so and so. He said, yeah, you bet. He worked hard.

He sure did, for himself.

What do you mean?

I just want to tell you, and I think you already know it, he absconded, he's handling money for three widows out in Mesa, and he was handling all of their funds and he milked them dry and these poor ladies are left with nothing. And you're going to appoint him to a responsible position to handle things of great value for the State of Arizona?

Yes. He worked hard for me and I'm not going to turn my back on him.

Governor, if you do that, I'm through with you —and I hung up on him. I was sizzling. I had no business hanging up on the Governor. I should have finished my sentence.

But all of a sudden, rubber was burning and horns were blaring and here comes that big black state car. And into my office flies, arms and feet flying, Governor McFarland.

You can't hang up on me and you can't talk to me like that.

I just did.

Tom. You know how hard . . .

I know how hard he worked. But he worked for himself. And I'm telling you, think about those women.

I'm going to appoint him and then you and I are through. Don't ever speak to me again and I won't speak to you.

This man really absconded with these women's money and left them penniless, and that's not right and you sure as hell shouldn't reward him.

Well, he stormed out of the office, I thought the door was going to fly off the hinges. We'd been friends for thirty years, I guess. Didn't speak to each other for two or three months. But he never did appoint him. Never.

Months later I ran into him one day, and we looked at each other like bulldogs and we both started smiling. He put his hand out, I put my hand out.

He was trying to be faithful, but it's wrong to appoint people that you know out of cronyism, it's not good government, and during the campaign this guy had said to me, what are you getting?

And I said, what do you mean, what am I getting? This was my first encounter with him.

He said, what are you getting? Everybody here wants something. You want something?

Wait a minute. Maybe you want something. I don't want anything.

Oh, come on. You don't put in these kinds of hours getting this man elected. You're working here eighteen hours a day and you're running your own business. What are you getting?

Absolutely nothing.

36

You mean to tell me you're doing this for patronage?

No. I'm doing it for two things: one for the State of Arizona and one because I like the Governor, he's a friend of mine and I think he'll be elected. But I don't want anything. And I'm not going to ask him for anything.

Well, you're nuts. Nobody works that hard.

So the guy didn't get the job, I'll tell you that.

◆

In all those campaigns I had a lot of help. Especially I had Joe Duke, he was sergeant-at-arms of the United States Senate. And I had Jimmy Minotto who was very astute in the ways of politics. I am not an expert on politics, but they ran their ideas by me, and I had the right to reject them or accept them.

I recall specifically when Senator McFarland ran against Barry Goldwater. Someone dreamed up the idea to revile Goldwater, to call him a soldier-of-fortune and a do-gooder. They called him Goldberger. And I rejected it all. No way, I said. It's a terrible thing to do in the first place, and the Goldwaters are good people, highly regarded. If you're voting for McFarland and somebody else is voting for Goldwater that does not mean that you have the right to be a character assassin. That's my decision. And I quit over it. I said, I won't be a party to this.

Well, it backfired on them. Barry Goldwater was elected and that's how he became Senator.

◆

Money was the easiest part in running a campaign. You didn't need much money in those days, you only needed 5 percent of what you need today.

First thing you do when you want to raise money, you put up your own. You cannot go out and raise money and expect other people to give if you're not willing to give yourself to whatever extent you can. Some people are bad money-raisers simply because they never give any money to their own candidate. You can't live in a community and have money and not give to a lot of things if you have any conscience at all. That opens doors for you for futures.

37

It was not hard to raise money. But here again, you did not need much. My candidates were outstanding and they were easy to elect. With Senator Hayden the last time, the biggest problem was he wasn't in town. I was caught up trying to elect a spook. I used to kid him. He was so busy in Washington, and he wasn't feeling well the last time. He was so highly regarded that we went back there and took some pictures to show back here, it was the early part of television, but even so, I think the money spent was very little. It's really a miracle he was elected. It really had nothing to do with Joe Duke or me or the rest of us. Just he was so highly regarded. He was the most powerful man in the United States Senate by far. Been there fifty years. He was a great man. An honest man. No way anybody could get to him for anything.

♦

Governor Mecham is not the first one to file a late financial report. I was the campaign manager once for O. L. McDaniel. I knew as much about running a campaign as you do about running this ranch — nothing. Anyway, I was his campaign manager and we probably spent four or five hundred dollars. That was a lot of money. Neither one of us had the money. He had a ranch at what is now Grand Avenue and Camelback. He had cattle and I had a little jewelry store. So we ran him and he got elected.

We were celebrating to beat hell and somebody tapped us on the shoulder one night at the Corinthian Room at the old Adams Hotel and said, did you guys file your papers?

I said, what papers?

They said, federal filing papers. You're supposed to have papers and you're supposed to file your expense statement. He may not be allowed into the Senate.

Oh God, so we scrambled, we found lawyers, we got information.

They said, all you have to do is file it and say you're late in filing.

Of course, the next day we did file it. It was no big thing. Actually, nobody had ever filed one. So it's not new. I suppose it's how you handle it. It's like President Nixon. If he hadn't lied, he'd have still been President full term. It was the lying and the cover-up that got the public, when he said to the public on the air, I'm no liar. I'm no crook. That's another story but if he'd of just said, yes, I knew all about it, the steam is gone, the story is gone, and they'd been doing dirty tricks like that to each other for years.

It always was open season during campaign. They'd either hire someone to go in there or they'd go in during the night. When I was running the campaign here for Senator Hayden, Senator McFarland, different ones, we had stuff taken. They'd have spies in our camp. We had spies in their camp. Someone would come to us voluntarily and tell us things that were going on and he was working for them. You'll always have professional politicians doing that.

39

All President Nixon had to do was tell the truth. It would have been over with.

◆

Governor Mecham didn't do anything that a lot of other people haven't done, but he got really scored on it simply because of personal unpopularity.

I think the same thing happened to Governor Mecham that happened to President Nixon. When you're in the public eye, the press are skeptics by nature, and when they think you've lied to them, they're going to turn heaven and earth to do something about it. That's what they believe they're put on this earth for, and they wouldn't be good journalists if they didn't. They don't hate Governor Mecham. I don't believe that. I don't think any of those people do. I don't think the guys hated President Nixon. I think if President Nixon had said, yes, we did that, it happens all the time, they've been doing it to us, too. The covering up is what cost him the presidency. I think that could be what happened to Governor Mecham. I know one thing, it's probably the worst thing that ever happened to Arizona. It's divided so many people.

And he's a religious, good man and it's too bad. I've known him ever since he came to Phoenix. Done business with him. Dealings are always straight-forward.

If the press is going to be free, they have to be responsible. To talk about the stockings of a Governor's wife, or the dress of a Governor's wife, is drabby, yellow journalism. And the paper that prints it is no better than the guy that writes it. They should not do it. I don't think they should talk about his wife. They certainly shouldn't say how tacky she is. And they're trying to make Willard Mecham look like a goof. He's not a goof, obviously. I'm sure they're decent, church-going men who made a mistake. It's too bad. It's bad for Arizona. Bad for everybody.

◆

I think candidates have turned too much to the so-called experts. And they really aren't experts. They really don't know what's going on. They know what they've been told is going on. But to be effective, if I wanted to run for office right now, I wouldn't go out of state and find me a group of people. I'd find somebody local. There's people here that could do the same thing any outsider can do.

I think Bruce Babbitt was beat to death by his advisers. His first speech he cussed the daylights out of and knocked the President of the United States. Well now, the President of the United States happens to be one of the most popular Presidents, particularly at that time, that we've ever had, even including President Kennedy.

Why would you make that many enemies the first rattle out of the box? Why can't you talk about taxes, freedom of the press, homes for the aged, health care, food, freedom, low-cost housing, safe automobiles, seat belts? There's a lot of things to talk about. Women or safety in the streets. Put patrolmen back on the street. The priority ought to be that a woman or a man should be able to go out and safely take a walk. And they can't. There's plenty to talk about. He didn't have to start knocking the President of the United States, who is very popular and who wasn't even running, so what did Babbitt have to gain? All he did was hurt himself. Every time you knock somebody, if they have two friends, you lose two friends. If they have a thousand — and President Reagan obviously had lots of friends. So he's saying to at least half or more of the United States, I don't like your man.

I think that's what knocked him out of the race. Bruce Babbitt is a very good man. He was an excellent Governor. He has a wife who's a great asset to him. And he could have made it. The press liked him. But he beat himself — he's the guy that hired those people out of New York. And I have a little trouble with a New Yorker trying to tell me how to sleep nights and what to eat, and I just don't think they've lived here long enough. Especially when they come in to do a campaign. They don't know. And they can hire all the people they want, I don't see anything wrong with hiring expert help, but at least the head and the main group should be Arizonans.

He was very successful with it before and Bruce Babbitt could have been the next President. I really believed it. But **41** when he started doing that, he lost me. I'm very fond of the Reagans as you know, and there's no need to pick at somebody who's not going to run anymore.

◆

It costs way too much for a person to run for office. They sell their soul. Way too much. I think there ought to be a limitation probably, but then again you're interfering with free commerce and you can't do that. But if you ring doorbells you can be elected to almost anything. Simply put, if you run in a district and there are 1,001 doorbells, families, and you ring 1,001 effectively and state your case, chances are you'll be elected. Unless you're upside down and ugly or something's wrong with you. But I think it's not hard to be elected if you're willing to put in the work. The trouble with ringing doorbells in Arizona, it's usually in August and in Phoenix it's awfully hot. It's very hard work. It would be hard work even in cool weather.

◆

As for running myself for political office, I don't have the appetite for it. It's flattering when people say they want to run you for office. It's very flattering. I was fortunate several times, friends came in and said, here's the money. We have all the money you'll ever want to spend. And we'll help you. You're electable. All the things show you are. And I said, you know the reason I'm electable is because I'm never running. And I want to keep it that way. They tried pretty hard, some pretty prominent people, I had an office full of them one time.

It would have been for Governor. I just said no. They had put up good money. They had all this stuff, all the facts and all the polls. Hell, at that time I was on forty committees. I suppose I was a do-gooder. I belonged to an awful lot of organizations trying to give something back to this community, really. It was fun. It was part of my business.

I wasn't that good myself. Channel 10 and KOOL radio were that good. We were in the midst of everything. It was easy to be a part of things. That's one of the reasons why they figured that they could elect me easily according to the polls. But it just wasn't me, I just wouldn't like it.

You know, you have more power out of office, by far. Absolutely. When you're in office you owe a lot of favors. That's distasteful to me. I think you should appoint the best man to do the job. By and large it does work out pretty well, but a lot of times some people are appointed that really shouldn't be.

I think that kids, the youth of America, have a point when they say that the adults don't set good examples. I think it's a lot of monkey-see monkey-do. Kids really believe that you have a lot more clout than you really do have. You don't have that much clout. If you get too far out of line as a politician, the public will take care of it. It does happen. Whoever invented this system knew what they were doing.

It's pretty hard to get away with anything in this community because the *Republic* and *Gazette* are vigilant and I have never believed for one minute that they have not been sincere in the things they look at, and now you have some other very good papers that are doing the same thing. You have the *New Times*; whether you like it or not, it's on top of things. And you've got Cox papers and you've got the paper up here in the north part of town. And the press will keep politicians honest.

I think this is very clean government here. Mostly it's clean. Really, it's clean because of the press. And I think most of the stations, the television and radio stations are vigilant in their watch, they've got a lot of people looking. And they're not afraid to tell about it.

Chapter 5

Making
the Movies

My brother George and I were on the Arizona Motion Picture Commission for probably forty years, and we spent a lot of time getting Hollywood film companies to come in to Arizona and spend a lot of money, a great deal of money, to make pictures here. We were appointed every year by the governor, and it was sort of automatic because we weren't political.

George got in with Tanner who had the limousine service in Tucson, and I knew the ranchers, where we could get land and cattle and horses and cowboys and extras.

It takes a lot of your time. The film people come to town and you spend thirty, forty, fifty days with them when they're making a movie on location. Martin and Lewis, one of their pictures was here. When you spend forty or fifty days with young, active guys like that, you're exhausted. They worked hard and they played hard, but they were terribly nice people. And it was a great non-polluting business that left a lot of money here. George brought in more movies than I ever could because he was better-liked and better-known in the movie industry. He was great friends with people like Orson Welles, Bill Holden, Walter Huston and John Huston, Alan Ladd. They all liked him and liked to make pictures down in Tucson.

The movie people conjured up an idea that George and I would represent them on a dollar-a-year basis. Course I don't think they ever paid us the dollar, come to think of it, but we represented Warner Brothers, Metro-Goldwyn-Mayer, anybody who was coming in, Universal Studios, Twentieth Century Fox, Paramount, and made a lot of pictures in this state. Our job was to find them cattle if they needed it, location, land, extras, buildings. A lot of stuff they would build and so we'd have to find a place that would work with them on a large scale. We built whole towns at times.

A lot of them came here and spent a lot of money, excellent for Arizona. The only fights we ever had were when I was trying to pull them to Phoenix and George was trying to pull them to Tucson and he was stronger than I was a lot of times. *Citizen Kane* was made down there but Walt Disney's *Song of the South* was made up here. I worked on it. I was with Walt Disney there for forty days and I've never even seen that movie.

We made an awful lot of pictures throughout those years. Several John Wayne movies. Gene Autry made a lot of movies here. Not the big expensive kind, you know, Gene's were more for kids. Wayne's movies were pretty high-budget. They spent lots of money. Old Tucson was built as a result of *Tucson, Story of Arizona*. They even built the whole town and actually took the bread line out of Tucson. That's the kind of money they spent. The extras would get thirty-five dollars a day and the average person in Tucson, a laborer working was getting only twenty dollars a week, fifteen dollars a week. So it was a good job and we used hundreds of them. They were there a long time.

Sedona, we got lots of movies in Sedona. Beautiful country. Monument Valley. The dunes out in the desert. The southern part of Arizona, very beautiful.

♦

James Howell was the head of the motion picture industry association and I did a lot of work with him. He was in Los Angeles and he wanted somebody over here to help him. Especially after a movie, *Road to China*. I've forgotten all the stars but it was a good picture, and we used the Apache Trail.

For it, we had a stunt up on the Apache Trail and they used a stunt man with a motorcycle, and he got hurt and he lay unconscious for months and months and months and months. It didn't look like he was ever going to come to. Well, in those days, a person hurt in Arizona got Arizona compensation after the accident. This was for an unlimited period, no maximum, at something like sixty or eighty percent of whatever he had been making. The stunt had been for thousands of dollars so he was being paid compensation of thousands of dollars a day.

The studios called me and they said, we need to talk to you. We are not going to come to Arizona again. The risk of financial exposure is too great. The stunt man accident was a terrible thing. We feel bad about it but it tells us that if we had a plane load or car load of these high-priced stars like William Holden and Walter Brennan, you name them, with their level of salaries, it would bankrupt the state because your law provides for compensation for an unlimited time. So we propose that if you want us to do more pictures that you get some kind of limit to the amount and length of time the state has to pay compensation.

45

We talked to some Senators and they said the only way you can do it is a Constitutional amendment and you've got to go to the people. So we worked like hell, my brother and myself, Oscar Giles, and we got help from Walter Bimson, Frank Snell, and raised some money and we passed the amendment to the Constitution that said compensation would not exceed $1,015 a month. Before it could have been $4,000,000 a day. We really worked on that and it passed by more than four-to-one. It's one of the model laws of the country now, and it has saved this country, Arizona. Immediately they started sending pictures back here.

◆

My work gave me a chance to meet all sorts of Hollywood stars. For instance:

Bing Crosby I knew quite well. My brother Jimmy lived with the Crosbys when he was working at Warner Brothers, which was across from Toluca Lake. This is in the late 1930s. And Crosby of course was at Paramount most of the time but he was in at Warner's once in a while, and he met my brother who was a kid learning the motion picture business. And he said, I have some kids about your age and I have some extra room at my house. How would you like to live with us? We'd like to have you.

They'd become acquaintances, friends. My brother moved in and lived with them for a while. And Crosby, I never saw him any time but what he was either whistling or singing. He was never silent. He would walk around Paramount Studios — in those days he had a house, Dotty Lamour had a house, and so did Bob Hope, right on the studio lot. Beautiful houses. Staffed. That was their home when they were shooting pictures. Because they worked God-awful hours.

They took my brother in just like one of the family. He lived with them for several years until he went into the service. Of course, he kind of grew up with those Crosby kids. They were all youngsters then. Jimmy was only fifteen or sixteen, and I think that's what Bing Crosby liked about him.

◆

I was with Walt Disney when he made a picture called *Uncle Remus' Song of the South.*

The greatest thing about that story is that Walt Disney would not allow tied-in clouds. That means glass shots. A glass shot is you come out here and take a picture of that building or that mountain and you put it on a big screen on a transparency and you put the scene in front of it and you shoot the scene. It obviously saves a lot of money and all, but Walt Disney, if he wanted clouds, he wanted real clouds.

We had a place down west of Phoenix called McDonald's Farm. We made it look like the South. We had the old trees and made a stream through it. And we'd go out every morning at 5:30 waiting for cumulus clouds. He wanted cumulus clouds, the big fluffy ones. And of course we didn't get them so we'd be there every day and he'd walk around, he had a slingshot and a pocketful of marbles and he was shooting them in the air. Thinking. And he was friendly and warm and nice and we'd eat lunch, be there, still waiting for clouds, it was forty-some days.

There was this one scene where a little dog had to cross the stream on a log, and he went to the middle and would stop and then he'd cock his head and go on. There was a guy there, the dog trainer, and he had pockets, dog pockets, looked like a big trench coat, and he had a puppy in every pocket. He was training them all. He smelled like a bunch of puppies. And of course everybody was laughing about the dog man, dog pockets.

They also had a horse they used in the scene, he was just a light horse, he wasn't very heavy, maybe 800 pounds. And they had a bunch of grooms, wranglers they called them, and they paid them a lot of money in this picture to just take care of the horses. Well, it came time to load the horse and they couldn't get it in. They had a van that was probably eight feet wide and a good ramp and they couldn't make it go up. They could have thrown the horse in if they wanted to. They couldn't load the horse.

So this little guy with the pockets came up to them and he says, do you want me to help you? And they laughed and they said, oh sure, and they handed him the shank of the horse and they were laughing like hell — this idiot that smells like a **47** dog and looks like a dog and talks like a dog. All he did was walk that horse about 100 feet with the rope, talking to him all the time. Now the wranglers had been hours walking that horse and had gotten nowhere. So here comes the "dog man" talking to that horse in his ear, patting him, and he walked him right into the van. These cowboys damn near all fainted. I saw this myself.

And that's the difference between brawn and brains. These guys really were sorry. These were cocky, arrogant cowboys. They were making more money, these were tough times, probably making $100 a day for wrangling. And they could not put it in because they had this horse upset, they had him angry.

This guy, that's all he did, walk 100 feet and talk to the horse, turned around and walked it right in. He says, you can close it up now. Then he and his dogs walked off into the sunset.

◆

Disney was a delightful man. He'd walk around and he'd think. I think every day he had a new idea and he was designing and building and he was never aloof. He was warm and friendly. He was a terribly nice fellow and it was costing him a fortune. Never shot a piece of film. He was waiting for just the right clouds. He was a perfectionist.

I've always believed that the only reason that the Disney company is still solvent is because of television. When television came along, he had been so much a perfectionist, and it cost so much to make his films and he had such a tremendous library, which he'd done on television, remember? They started out with the Disney hour. He sold those films and that kept him solvent. Of course he went on from there and they still have a fantastic library.

♦

Irene Dunn. I was in the jewelry business. I think she and Spencer Tracy were making a movie. She would come into the store and look at things and she bought a gift for someone in there. And we became acquainted. A very lovely, delightful, quiet, beautiful lady. And she was here quite a while. She was a great friend of Mrs. Davis, Nancy Reagan's mother. Of course, we had mutual friends.

Clark Gable came here quite often, stayed at the Biltmore or at a friend's house. He came here primarily to bird hunt, vacation. He loved to go dove hunting, quail hunting. And he was very enamored with a young lady by the name of Betty Chisholm who had a home in the Biltmore and they were very close friends. She was a lovely gal, still is. She still lives in the Biltmore. But he met a lady, somebody in the interim, and he married her and all of a sudden we were all shocked because all of us that knew them felt that they were going to get married, Betty Chisholm and Clark Gable. What happened I never knew and I never asked.

Alan Ladd was married to a gal named Sue Carroll. They were both at Paramount. Very fine actor. Actually, he wore lifts in his shoes and he was short.

Dottie Lamour was a dear friend, still is. She's about my age. Absolutely gorgeous. Absolutely humble. Absolutely plain. She had a beautiful home right in the lot at the studio. Always a lady. Always nice. Married a fellow named William Howard III from Boston or someplace. Had a couple of kids. Named one Tommy, Tom. She's just a dear friend. A fine actress. Loving, beautiful, and a nice gal. We've stayed friends over the years.

Pat O'Brien was probably the most fun man I've ever known. I spent months with him when he was here doing *Ring of Fear*, something like that. Circus-type show or something. He

48

lived at the Adams, I lived at the Adams. He was a great story-teller. Also a great conscience and a great heart.

He said to me one time, this is four or five o'clock in the morning, he says, I need a ride to the Convent of the Good Shepherd. I promised the sisters I'd come out and talk to the kids. Will you take me out there in the morning?

I said, do you know what time it is now? We'd been up all night.

Yeah, he says, but I got to go. Will you take me out?

So I drove him out to the Convent of the Good Shepherd. Of course, the sisters are all standing at the front of the gate waiting to see him. They'd known him before. And he told them stories, all clean, had them laughing, rolling, right in the front. **49** Then we went inside and he got hold of those kids and he spellbound them for an hour, just talking. The gift of gab, it was just marvelous.

And I said, Pat. We were heading back. I said, that's nice of you. You were up half of the night. It was our stupid fault, not theirs. But you went out there and you made the sisters feel good. You made those kids feel good.

He says, what else is there? That's what you're supposed to do. I don't get any credit for that.

Donald O'Connor was at Paramount, as I was. He was an actor and a very successful one. And Paramount had the old Marion Davies house down at Santa Monica. Beautiful old place. All those artifacts that William Randolph Hearst brought back from Europe. Gorgeous home. Marble, granite, just a beautiful place. And I wanted to go over and take my children. The kids were little and I was looking for a place and Paramount said, come and use our house. Well, the house turned out to be the Marion Davies house. In the other end of it was Donald O'Connor with his kids. He was also by himself. A delightful guy. He was just a nice man, easy to be around, like most of those people. This was thirty, forty years ago. The house is now torn down, but it was a lavish, gorgeous place, and it was nice of them. Where do you take kids at that age? They were youngsters. Of course, they had a wonderful time.

Every time Tex Ritter came to town you'd hear that boom-ing voice out in the TV station reception area. Is Tom here? And he'd sit down and we'd just talk about old times. He was a delightful, genuine, kind, warm man with talent. Huge, mammoth. He'd always come in and we'd talk for maybe an hour or two. Never had an appointment. Never said when he was coming, he'd just show up. Of course I'd put everything aside and we'd sit and visit. Delightful. Fun to have him.

Kenny Rogers called me several times over the years. He wanted to get horses and I never did anything about it because I was always afraid things would go sour. Next thing I know, a year or two later he had bought a horse and he said, would you come and look at my horse in Athens, Georgia? Some people had gotten hold of him and sold him some horses and I think he had bad advice, frankly, and he was way down in Athens, Georgia where you couldn't get much expertise.

So we have a plane and I took our doctor and my wife, several people, and went down there. He put us up beautifully. He had a fantastic place, rolled curb gutters, lawns. It was unbelievable. Huge indoor area. Lavish, gorgeous place. Indoor swimming pool for horses. Awful waste of money, but gorgeous. And he had sitting out in the middle of the arena, he had a thing with swivel chairs so I didn't have to turn around. He had it just deluxe. A snack bar set out there in the middle.

We looked at all these horses and we visited and talked and I liked him. I liked her. Nice people. And I was surprised that I liked the stud, because I'd heard how he'd been gypped on the stud. Really, the only thing wrong with this stud, he was too small and Rogers had paid a lot of money for him.

We went into lunch after we looked at the horses and I admired this eagle that was sitting in his living room. The following Christmas I got a call, could you come to the airport with some men? It was Kenny Rogers. He says, Merry Christmas, and he gave me that eagle.

About then the horse business started a down turn but we've remained good friends since. I'm very fond of him. He's almost out of the horse business now. He took up photography and he's very good at that. I think he's one of the best natural talents that ever lived. And a nice guy. I was glad to be a friend to him.

50

Norma Shearer. A similar situation — mutual friends. Lovely lady. Probably knew her through the Reagans, I don't remember. Absolutely gorgeous. Terribly lovely. Just easy to talk to, easy to know.

♦

I knew Elizabeth Taylor years ago. And I hadn't seen her in years until I had a call, they wanted me to help. They said, we're having a problem raising money. And Elizabeth Taylor has been, right from the beginning, a very strong supporter of the fight against AIDS, trying to get help, funds. And a lady in the horse business I know came to me and said, Mr. Chauncey, will you consider helping us with AIDS? We need help badly and we're not going anywhere. We have a place to do a show, Elizabeth Taylor has a huge crowd of people from CATS, and we'll have a great show but we don't have many tickets sold.

And they said, we'd also like you to give Queen Bask, which is a great mare.

I said, that's an awful expensive gift.

And she said, well, it's for a worthwhile cause.

I was sitting here one day and Dr. Eugene LaCroix calls me and he says, Tom, we're going to have to cancel the show. We've got all this great show and we've sold no tickets. It was like a Friday and the show was on Monday. And he was actually crying.

Will you help?

I said, just calm down. I'll be over there. He's just two miles around the corner. So I went over and he was terribly upset.

He said, we've got all these arrangements made, all the expenses, and I've given the facilities and we've got all these things hired. We have no tickets sold. And they were expensive tickets. And we needed 1,000 people, and we only had three or four days. So I'm going to cancel it.

I picked up the phone and I called JoAnn Ralston who has a public relations agency here in town. I've known her for years. I said, Joannie, first of all, they couldn't get any press. They got no press at all. Something was awry about AIDS, I

don't know where the money went, they weren't getting anyplace. So I said, Joan, would you help me? Do you know the
story about AIDS?

She said, nobody knows the story about AIDS. There's
nothing being done about it.

I said, would you consider a crash program? See if you
can get us some press, help us work it out?

And she said, yes.

I said, I'll pay you for it. They don't have any money. If
you'll get your people together and see what you can do.

And I turned to Dr. LaCroix and I said, we'll get the
crowd and we can get the tickets sold. Of course, he heaved a
52   big sigh of relief. And she did go to work and she did get press
and we filled the room. I think I bought thirty or forty tickets.
They were $1,000 a piece for the ones that I had. And I gave a
horse. It cost me an awful lot of money and, much to my disgust,
I found out that 85 percent of that money went to Elizabeth
Taylor's group. It didn't go to AIDS at all. It all was a terrible
mess, but we did have a crowd and without a doubt, the finest
show that's ever been put on in Arizona. They had Elizabeth
Taylor, George Hamilton, a lot of the people from CATS. It was
a great evening. Beautifully done.

But I gave them too much, I guess. Makes you wonder
why you give anything. I was the largest contributor in cash of
anybody in the place. I think it cost me out-of-pocket about
$50,000 for tickets, airplanes and public relations and the stuff
I did for them. Plus the horse. Crazy.

◆

Franchot Tone. I met him, God, it seems like 100 years
ago. Franchot Tone came here to do a movie. I can't even remember the name of the movie. Of course he stayed at the
Adams Hotel where I was. And we were helping get locations
and it was kind of an eerie movie. It was unfortunate. Franchot
Tone was a lovely man, a great actor, but they had a rough time
making the movie. I don't know all the details, but I liked him
very much. A fine actor, a nice man. And a lot of people go on
location and they think it's a good time to party, I guess. The
picture was not very successful.

Of course, Spencer Tracy was the king of all of them. A gal who lived here in town went to work as his secretary. She was with him until he died. She'd been a secretary here in town, we were kids together and she was great with him and of course he had a great love affair with Katie Hepburn. I knew Spencer mostly because I doubled in a movie for him. He made a picture, it was either *God is My Co-Pilot* or *G.I. Joe*, I've forgotten which, down at Luke Field and we went out every day for a couple of months to suit up and wait to get the right clouds. And he was either a major or a colonel, I've forgotten, and I doubled for him. I was cheaper than the regular doubles, I think. But that movie had Spencer Tracy, Lionel Barrymore, maybe Irene Dunn, I'm not sure who all was in it.

53

What I did in doubling were scenes of walking into a cloud, not much. A very small part, but it was enough that it was a lot of work. They asked me to do it. I had white hair like he did and about the same stature, and they wanted to shoot this picture. We went out there every day for a couple months, 5:30 in the morning, and rather than bring an extra over or someone special, I was there anyway with them. I was liaison for the studio and the military and the state. So they said, wear a uniform.

We had a young fellow by the name of 2nd Lt. J. J. McDonald, who was a nice kid and I liked him very much. And he was partly assigned to us. They flew some of the planes for the stunts, and they had a new aircraft arrive, I've forgotten what it was, acrobatic, and he kept looking at me and I'm in that major or colonel uniform, with the hat and the whole bit, waiting.

He says, why don't we take a ride in one of those new airplanes?

I said, oh no. Tracy can't get one of those airplanes, they're brand new.

You can, he said.

What do you mean I can?

He said, look at your shoulders. You're somebody.

I said, you're nuts.

He said, come on, we can get an airplane. We were on the flight line anyway, he says, come on. Crazy kid, and I had no business doing it. We walked up and everyone is saluting me like a real officer.

I'd like an airplane, take a ride.

Yes sir.

They rolled this new plane out, and me and this McDonald get in it.

Worst mistake I ever made in my life.

He gets me up in the air and he's doing outside loops, inside loops, Immelmanns, stalls, dead stick, you name it. He did everything. I was about to throw up every two minutes. And I got back on the ground and I was wobbly. And I called him everything I could think of. He had me up there thirty minutes. We were going through the clouds and under the clouds. Just awful.

54

♦

Wayne, the Duke as they called him, John Wayne was very outgoing and had a lot of acquaintances. Knew a lot of people. And was always active in everything around him. He'd go into a town, he'd see something that was needed, he'd quietly donate or do something. He was just a nice man. Later in life he made most of his own pictures. It was his company. But with Wayne it was just what you see is what you got. That's the way he was. Loved horses and a pretty good rider.

Wayne took me for a ride one time I'll never forget.

It was on a ranch that I have now that then was his favorite place, it was called 26 Bar Ranch. It's up at Springerville. A beautiful ranch. And it's big. With Winslow we would run probably 3,000 head of cattle. They're large ranches, both of them.

We were up in the summer, and there's meadows and streams and elk and antelope. It's just a gorgeous place. Big vistas. Big meadows. Aspen trees. The biggest aspen trees I've ever seen. And that ranch runs from 6,000 feet up to about 9-10,000 feet, so you have a lot of climbs.

I went up there about twenty-five or thirty years ago, and we were having a field day for the kids. Youth day. Cattle day. Of course, they had the great herd of cattle. 26 Bar was a great ranch, and Wayne owned it with a fellow named Louis Johnson, also a nice man. Still lives here.

Anyway, he said, come on. I'll give you a ride. And he had a car out there, and I don't know if you saw the movie *Hatari! Hatari!* had those cars with the cutout like a turret so you could stand up and look out at the animals. He had one of those cars up there and we got into that. Gordon Paulsen was there with me. I was in the front seat and there's a dirt gravel road, it's paved now, and you're winding down like a snake and by the side, no guard rails, it's several hundred feet straight down.

All of a sudden this son of a bitch Wayne jumps out through that turret and lands on his feet and the car is still going. I'm grabbing for the wheel, I finally pulled to the side of the road with it.

He'd seen some wild turkeys and he ran just like a monkey and swooped up a rock and was throwing it at the turkeys, he didn't get any, but that's the way they catch the birds in Mexico that they send up here. They stun them. They throw a handful of rocks and they bring in the birds.

Well, fortunately, I grabbed the wheel and I got the damn car stopped. I wanted to kill him. I said, I'm going back home, now. I'm not going up this mountain. I'm not going anyplace with you. You're nuts. And he was laughing, of course.

He didn't see anything unusual about it. He just wanted to go chase those turkeys. He was running around like a deer. He was driving the car and literally just jumped right up through that turret, that open space they made them with so you could drive into the elephants and game and tigers and all and be safe. He thought it would be fun. He was agile as hell. Of course, this was almost thirty years ago, too. But that car was going maybe twenty, thirty miles an hour on a curved mountain gravel road that was sloping all over the place. The car was going every which way. It's a miracle we didn't go off that mountain. I pulled it into the other side of the road and got it stopped. And I'll tell you, I had to go home to get some new underwear. It scared the hell out of me.

But he was a delightful man and it's a thrill to have that ranch. It's a great ranch. Streams. Lakes. Rivers. Beautiful. Great cattle.

♦

We started the first unit of the Academy of Motion Picture Arts in Arizona, and I was a voting member. I was president of it, I guess. Some of my friends in Hollywood wanted a unit here, the studios and the people in the art industry asked me to form one and I did. I was in it for quite a while and I quit it because I didn't like the way they politick. There's so much of that. Tremendous ads to promote so-and-so for an Oscar. They ought to give it to so-and-so because she's older than somebody else. You know, those kinds of campaigns.

I respect all of them that get up there; they're awfully good, let's face it, awfully good. But some really good ones never make it because others don't like them. It's a popularity contest. They just don't like the star personally. And there'd be group voting, block voting where a bunch of employees get together and get one guy to say, here, we're all voting for so-and-so, we hope you'll join us.

It often runs down to popularity. Get enough votes. There's a lot of campaigning goes on. They promote too much. Too much hype. Often it has nothing to do with who's best. And I just thought that it ought to be more than that. I'm not sure they even look at all those pictures. I know I didn't have time to.

Chapter 6

Broadcasting

I had absolutely no plans to get into broadcasting but things happened.

I was in the jewelry store in the Adams Hotel. Gene Pulliam came along, Gene Autry came along. Gene Autry was taking up flying lessons here in town from a fellow by the name of Bill Marsh. He and Ina, Autry's wife, stayed at the Adams for months while Gene got a license. Then he went in the service.

Gene Pulliam came to town and at the time owned WIRE in Indianapolis and several other radio stations. We became acquainted and he wanted to meet some people in town. On a confidential basis, he told me he was trying to buy the *Republic* and the *Gazette*.

I had a friend by the name of Thomas Lincoln Kerney, who owned the *Trenton Times*, in Trenton, New Jersey. So Tom Kerney, Clarence Budington Kelland, an agency man, Gene Pulliam, Gene Autry all became stockholders of the *Republic* and *Gazette*, the Phoenix newspapers. And Bruce Barton, they were the principals.

M.C. Reese, an insurance man, had a radio station in Phoenix and Gene Autry, we were making pictures and Gene said we ought to buy a station. Gene was always anxious to be in radio. He thought it was a great medium. He thought it was going to be very successful. And he wanted to be in it and he said, we ought to buy that radio station. Will you run it?

I said, no. I don't know anything about running a radio station.

Well, he said, you could oversee it, but you ought to be in it because you're known, you're local, and we're going to get a license. We're going to have to have somebody local that's well known and liked in the community or the commission won't give us a license. Will you go in with us?

I finally said, sure. So we bought the station. For partners we had people like A.G. Atwater of the Wrigley company. Rex Schepp from Indianapolis prior to A.G. Atwater. Jack Kane and John Rockwell from the Adams. We also put a station on the air in Tucson, one in Yuma, one in Nogales. The station cost quite a bit. We had to spend a lot of money on it. We built a studio. At that time the studio was over by Buckeye Road, but we moved it up to the Adams. I was supposed to eventually have majority control, but I never did. Some of them got out. Some of them quit. They didn't like it. It was losing too much money. I didn't know what the hell I was doing, frankly. But we hired good management and then things happened and we sold that station and bought KOOL.

We sold the first station to John Mills, who owned the Westward Ho, and a fellow named Mullins. We got out of that one, and Gene said, if you'll take this other one, you can take whatever you want of this other one and I'll go ahead and buy it, and so he bought KOOL. Then we, or that same group, applied for a television station. We didn't know what the hell we were doing, but we applied anyway. Nobody knew. It was a dream.

Gene Pulliam became very unenamored with the Federal Communications Commission. And he told me, I'm going to get out of the radio business. I don't want any part of it. I don't want the government telling me how to tell a story, or whatever. And he said, I'm not going to be subjected to that anymore. He got out here and out of the Vincennes, Indiana, station; WIRE in Indianapolis he sold to his former employees, and he just completely got out of broadcasting. He said the day will come when the government will be too heavy-handed. And he said you can't have a free press with somebody in Washington telling you how to run anything. He said, I just don't want to be in that position. He was very adamant about it.

58

I begged him not to do it. He was a good partner. But he said, no way. He just got out. He was a good newspaperman but he sure didn't want anybody in the government telling him how to run a newspaper. He just wouldn't do it.

◆

At the beginning of radio, how the CBS network came to Phoenix is a story in itself.

Early on, Phoenix got CBS because Mr. William Wrigley Sr. used to come here, and he had his house on the hill and he couldn't get his radio programs. He had sponsored a lot. He was a tremendous sponsor of radio. And he was complaining bitterly that he couldn't get the CBS network, he couldn't hear his shows. So I took it upon myself to call the network and said, we've got to have a line in here.

59

Well, they said, it costs too much money, you don't have that many people there, it won't serve that many people, it's not economical.

I said, how much money does Mr. William Wrigley spend with you?

Oh, they said, my God.

I said, I think the line ought to be in tomorrow, don't you?

And they said, yes, we sure do.

Because, I said, he's going to be on the hill trying to tune in those programs, and you better have them in here. You guys better get off your ass and get this line in.

It went to KOY, and that's how it got there, because Mr. Wrigley couldn't hear his programs. The line was costly, but they found it real quick, the next day.

That helped build KOY. That was the beginning of them becoming a quality station because they had all of those shows. I think they had four or five shows sponsored by Mr. Wrigley.

(KOY had gotten its start in a place across the street from the Westward Ho called Nielsen Radio and Sporting Goods, 621 N. Central. Nielsen had a bowling alley and the sporting goods store, so in a corner of the building, in one small room, he built a radio station and started KOY.)

◆

Two things I wouldn't tolerate on any stations I had anything to do with.

One was liquor. You cannot be on the air and not be responsible. A drunk has no business on the air talking to kids and women, children and mothers and fathers, and having a voice that's important. You have no right to do that. You need all your faculties. Liquor does not belong on the air no matter how good you are, and if you find somebody doing it, they should be taken off the air. That isn't to say you won't try to dry them out or that you won't try to help them. But they're off the air as of that minute. And then you go ahead and try to help them but if they ever take a drink and you know about it, they're gone. You can't have liquor on the air. If they want to get drunk that's their business. But they're not going to get drunk there. I just said, you're through. Pick up your check.

I also wouldn't tolerate profanity. You're going into a lot of people's homes as their guest and you're teaching kids. Profanity is a crutch for an angered mind. In my opinion, brilliant minds don't need profanity. They use very lovely words to express themselves. We all fall on profanity sometimes, but it certainly isn't our best shot, is it?

You should use proper grammar at all times on the air because children learn from what they hear. If we were very careful in what we say on the air and it's proper grammar, we'll all have a better place, better understanding, better communications.

◆

(Editor's Note: Some of his closest associates of the past 40 years shared their special insights into Mr. C. Here's the first.)

Bill Lester (seventeen years station manager of KOOL-AM-FM): When I went from KOY to Tom's radio stations, KOOL-AM-FM, they both were losing money. And then I presumed to suggest we add another $100,000 a year expense by staying on the air twenty-four hours a day and by adding expensive staff. He just said go ahead without blinking an eye. He wanted to be Number One and I told him this was the way to do it.

He said to me, Willy, listen. If you serve the best and you take care of your listeners, don't worry. The money will come. He said it before I did. I didn't have to keep pounding at the boss, saying, will you give me money to do this, can I do that? He said, you do what's right and build the station that serves the public and, Bill, the money will come.

Well, it did. At the end of just thirty days we had the FM station out of the red. It took seven months or so with AM, but we did become the Number One station and people just naturally tuned to us, day or night, to find out what was going on.

I found out he was very like Irish people. They say the Irish have a sense of something with people. He was remarkable in how he believed in his associates. Quick to love, sensitive to your emotions and your feelings, like the Irish.

One time, Tom was furious that one of our top executives in radio passed him in the little narrow hall and blew a martini breath in his face. And he was instantly angry and lost his temper and called Homer in, his executive, he called me in, his VP, and he said, now Willy, listen to me. So-and-so had been drinking at lunch. Now you know one thing we don't do in this company and everybody knows it, you don't have a martini lunch so you go out and get him out of here. Get him his check, I want him out right now.

I said, well, okay, but. . . .

And he was still angry that somebody violated the code and had been drinking.But let me tell you. When I said, but . . . — he gave me the biggest gift you could give a person because he listened to me and said, what is it?

I said, what if I haven't made it plain to John that he can't do it? Then that's partly my fault and I don't feel good about it, but I'll go over and I'll take him over right now and get his check or —.

Or what?

Or I could take him over across the street for a cup of coffee and just say to John, just in case you didn't understand, we have a rule around here and that is, if you want to take a drink at lunch, you're through. That's just like coming and signing your resignation to me. So I have to say to you, don't take a drink at lunch unless that's your word to me that you've just resigned. Tom said, well go ahead. Go ahead, but I don't want to ever do that with him again.

So I just said to John, John, the rule around here is we don't drink at lunch. Buy one for your guest if you want to. Buy him two or three. Nobody cares. But we don't do it. What you do tonight when you go home is your business, but not on the job.

I did that with John who was older than I, very good at what he did, terribly good, and I just really said, John, I'm not even going to say, promise me you won't do it again. I'm just gonna say I've got to stand on this. We gotta do it this way, John, old buddy, old pal. He says, oh yeah, yeah, yeah, I do.

He made it through another year, year and a half to retirement and we had a retirement party for him. Now who do you think was just proud as a peacock of all the years that John had worked for him? Tom. Tom was so glad that John made it.

Another time Tom came to my desk and was just so excited about the impact of the two radio stations. He was pleased and he was proud to have somebody come up and say what a great thing the staff did for our community affairs. Or when a lady came up and said, do you realize that one of your guys ran a little announcement for us that the food bank was running out of money and that if anybody in the off season would like to make their Christmas donation now to keep the doors open, please call Helen somebody with a phone number? And an executive at Motorola called her up, he was in his car and heard that announcement and gave her $10,000, years ago when that was a lot of money. That lady just got in tears.

◆

Tom Chauncey: Eventually I was putting our television station on the air. It was quite a struggle at one time because I also had cattle and the jewelry store.

What people don't realize is that in those days television stations were there for the wanting. All you had to do was apply. Nobody wanted them. And there was no pattern to go by. Any other business you can go in any given town and learn something. Radio wasn't so bad, there was something to go by. But when it came to television, my mistake was having friends in Hollywood, because we tried to do things like programming and stuff in Phoenix like Hollywood did. Of course, they knew how to make pictures but they did it so expensively. Copying them, I introduced bad practices and salaries.

I guess what I did best was work hard. Eighteen hours a day. I stayed there. I'd go down at four or five in the morning and I'd be there until midnight. I built the station myself because I didn't know any better, saved us a lot of money. Found an old building. I criss-crossed Phoenix in a car, north, south, east, west, looking for a location and I also had to look for a place on a mountain for the tower. I found on West Adams one of the buildings. We have the whole block now. There had been an auto dealership, the place was empty and it was cheap and I bought it. Paid cash for it and built the station and put it on the air. After we applied for the license, Gene and I, KOY applied for the same channel and we would have had to go to a hearing in Washington, so we did an experiment. We joined hands with Channel 10 and it was KOY and KOOL, the licensees, a joint experiment. We'd alternate days. Even tried to use some of the same staff.

63

One day Jack Williams and Al Johnson came to me from KOY and said, Tom, we're going broke with this thing.

And I said, so are we. We're in terrible shape.

They said, would you buy it? I said, yeah. If you come up with a price I'll try to buy it. And I've forgotten how much it was.

They said, we want out. We're losing our butts. And I don't know whether you can get any money; we can't.

I said, I think we can get the money if you want. I think it will be good someday. It's not good now, I realize that.

So they said, we want out. We'll take so much, whatever it was.

I went to Walter Bimson and he gave me the money and I paid them and we became one station. We started making money shortly after that. But it was a long haul. They were good people and we were both in trouble. We both knew a lot more about radio than we knew about television, which was nothing.

We rode the network as much as we could in the beginning. They had the best programming and they were very helpful to me. That's where I learned to like the people at CBS. We became very close friends. Gene had known them for years. Gene did radio shows for them. That's really how I got in with CBS.

Most of the TV station owners had partners to help with the finances. Banks and institutions would not loan, insurance companies would not loan on broadcasting groups. You couldn't borrow money to go into television. They thought it was a loser. There was only one that I knew of and it was Jefferson Standard Life Insurance Company in Greensboro, North Carolina, who did loan money because their people were far-seeing and I knew them through other friends and did borrow some money from them and helped other stations borrow money. Of course, we ate it up twice as fast. We all underestimated what TV would cost. Just the basic tubes for a camera in those days were $6-8,000 apiece.

Friendship is so important in life. There was a Leslie Atlas who was the head of Chicago West for CBS. The czar of network radio. He didn't think much of television, didn't think it would work. When he finally got in TV it cost him twice as much as if he had gone in with both feet.

He was at WBBM-TV and they had some Dumont cameras and then they bought some new RCA cameras and he gave the old ones to me. That's how we started. We couldn't afford new cameras. We didn't have the money.

They would send their tubes they had used on the network, all bright and new. It saved us a fortune in tube operating costs the first year. Real friendly.

We still lost $60,000 or more a month on our TV station in Phoenix and some more on our sister station in Tucson. That was a million bucks a year and if it hadn't been for Walter Bimson at the Valley Bank we wouldn't have been in business. Nobody else would lend to us. No question about it. I went to see Walter I think four or five times in one week and borrowed money to make the payroll. And he said, will this work? I said, Walter I can tell you. It will work. It's going to turn the corner. We used to sit and dream it was going to make a great vehicle, and I was sure it was going to make money. And Walter Bimson was a far-seeing, visionary, lovely man. I said, absolutely.

Finally I got to where I was ashamed to go to Walter anymore. We always paid the interest but payrolls were atrocious. Everything was atrocious. We were losing money like drunken sailors.

At that time I had a friend by the name of W.T. Waggoner, Jr. from Texas, an oil family with something like 3,300 wells, a very dear friend.

He looked at me one day and he said, what's the matter with you?

I said, nothing.

Yes there is something. What's the matter with you?

It's kind of tough right now.

What's tough?

Payroll and all this crap. It's killing me trying to keep this thing going. I'm about to lose the station. My partners won't put any more money in here. Some of them have dropped out, I don't blame them. It just isn't popular — television. And I hate to go back to Walter Bimson. I've borrowed so damn much money over there.

What would it take to save it?

God, I don't know. Five or six hundred thousand.

Why can't I loan it to you?

I don't know. Why can't you?

He said, what do you want? Tell me, what is it? I told him whatever it was and he said, no problem, and made the check out to me, right then and there, $500,000 or $600,000. Just like that.

I said, wait a minute. You can't do that. I might lose all of this.

I don't care. I'd rather have you alive than dead. You look terrible.

So I said, okay. Draw something up and I'll pay you off in five years.

He says, you don't have to pay it off that soon. How about ten years or something? Set up an indenture or something.

So help me, in three years I paid it all off with interest. But without him and without the Valley Bank, there would have been no KOOL radio and television as it's known today. We couldn't of done the kinds of things that we did. I'd have lost everything I had in it. So would Gene Autry. So would all the partners we had. And a lot of them did get out. Just took the money and left. A lot of my partners fell by the wayside. But Gene stayed in. I stayed in. And finally, it did turn the corner.

What made the difference? Acceptance, sets, knowledge. And we had learned how to operate it better. Getting CBS, and learning, and acceptance of television all made it work. And it made money ten times as fast as it ever lost it once it got going.

We paid our bills. It was a mint. It made money like it was going out of style. That had nothing to do with my genius or anything. It was just a fact of life that television caught on. And it really did catch on. But up till then it was pretty bleak.

66

◆

After a couple of years, I had to go down to the station and run it. It got so big. You have to remember about television — there were no archives you could reach back into, no place you could go and learn. You had to play it by ear and learn and grow. And I found I hardly ever got to the jewelry store. So finally, big companies were after the store name. It was a good name. I said, no. I don't want my name splattered all over the rest of my life and watch it be somebody else's Tom Chauncey Jewelers, so I just won't sell it. I closed it up, had a sale and got out of it.

The last person I depended on so much, I went to her funeral a few days ago, was Billie Sorlie. And she was the one who really ran it. The last few years when I was so involved in television, she was marvelous. She really was as responsible, or more so, than I was, for the jewelry store. A very super person, a good lady.

◆

People used to kid me about my office at the TV station. It was huge. It was about fifty feet long, something like that, and probably thirty or forty feet wide. The reason it was so big is because it was the easiest way to build it. I bought an old store building and a bowling alley next to our building. We needed space and rather than spend all the money to put in walls and everything, we took the front end which had been a restaurant and a reception area and all that and just put wallpaper on it and finished it and carpeted it and it made a gorgeous office. The ceiling had the old tin plates.

It was an old, old building. It was in No. 1 of the town sites in Phoenix, the first development of any kind in the city of Phoenix. And so the building was really old.

The office was big because it was cheaper to do it that way. They just put a false ceiling in it it and it was a beautiful office. We closed the windows off for noise because we used it for shooting a lot of interviews. And we had meetings in there. It really was a mini art museum as it turned out.

One of the fixtures in that office came from Gene Autry. He always had pretty good large offices and you'd go in Gene's office and in the corner of the room was this lifelike wooden Indian. You would always say hello to him, of course. I admired him so one year Gene sent one over to me. He's all hand-made and he walks. He's put together so that you can pick him up and walk him. I've had him about forty years.

He has joints in his knees and you can move him and set him up. That's why I set him up in the corner of my own office at the ranch. He reads the *Wall Street Journal*, checking his investments.

◆

We had a family at Channel 10. It was a real family place. That fellow you saw that just came in, I was telling my daughters about him last night. His name is Dale Vailencourt. Dale Vailencourt retires tomorrow, twenty-six years. He came out of the military and went to work for us. He was an engineer. Quiet, unassuming, had a little chip on his shoulder, not much.

We had never been unionized, but the union did come in and unionized the engineers, which was a national trend, and they asked me about it and I said, if you want to be union that's all right with me. I don't care. And I didn't try to stop it. I didn't discourage it. I did say, one thing you better remember, if you have a union like Hollywood, you're not going to have jobs, none of us, because you can't have a guy stand by just to plug in a cord like they do in Hollywood. Neither will you have apprentices and learning.

But I said, I'm not going to stop you and I'm not going to discourage it. If you want to have a union, go right ahead. Well, they didn't do it that time but later on they did. And Dale was the shop steward, he represented the union. He came to see me and I never had a moment's trouble with him. He'd come in and he'd say, can you do so and so? And I'd say, yes or no. Most of his requests were helpful. Things that should be done, like a water fountain ought to be in the back where they're walking to the front and wasting time, or they ought to have a place to put their stuff, because people are stealing their valuables.

68   Television was new. It wasn't a business like a grocery store or a restaurant where you could go see how it worked. We didn't know what we were doing. So most of the times he came in it was helpful, and he and I never had an argument. We never had a problem. In fact, it was easier because they would negotiate the wages and they were fair. They weren't easy, but they were fair.

◆

Phoenix is now the 20th largest TV market in the country. When we went on the air it was maybe the 100th. It was also one of the best stations in the United States. The bellwether station. High regard. High respect. I had a limitation to the amount of commercials we'd run and I would allow no profanity on the air. None. We previewed a lot of stories, if I knew there was a dirty word, we'd bleep it. I don't think it belonged on the air. I think there are some things I would probably allow now that I didn't then, but I cut a lot of things out. And it must have been worth something because we were Number One, and highly regarded.

◆

I did everything at the station except I would not go on the air. I did everything else. News took most of my time. I always believed that news was the best thing television could do locally. And that was my dream — to build the best news station in the country.

I managed, hired, fired, programmed, scheduled, the whole bit. It was strictly hands-on, day to day. We were the only station in the country at the time doing an editorial every day. Sometimes we did two editorials, but we did them every day. It was probably the best thing we did. They were tough to do. I insisted they be a minute or less in time. I would never let them be very long. Maybe two minutes if they had a really good story. But, we kept it short. And I think it was reasonably successful. We ended up the most successful news department in the state in electronics. And were well known throughout the country.

◆

Explicit sex I wouldn't allow on the air of any station. I'm not a prude, but I don't think it belongs there. I remember fighting pay television tooth and hammer, saying that they'll use the excuse that they're not over the air, that they're on cable and that they will not run commercials, they're going to charge for it and there would be no commercials, no sponsorship. Repeated it time after time after time. They just simply lied to the people. And obviously, they're using explicit sex.

It's just like the phone companies that allow these porn stories going over the air. It's a disgrace to that company that goes out and buys classical music and plays great things to create a great impression and then allows these kids to have this filthy, vile stuff. They don't need it. All they have to do is say no.

There's no room in the world for explicit sex on the air. There's no room on the air for filth because you're going into a home. Your children are looking at it. My children. My grandchildren. Your grandchildren. And broadcasters have an obligation. We're supposed to educate and help. You're not supposed to teach the dirty words and filthy practices.

The bottom line was fine when we didn't have them. We did very well indeed. If we were doing so bad running a clean station, how come everybody wanted it? Filth and pornography don't help on the bottom line. They hurt on the bottom line. They drive people away and if they keep it up, television as we know it will not be here. They're going to break themselves because people don't have any respect for them.

◆

Gene Autry and I had a wonderful relationship for thirty-five or forty years. Then he hocked the TV station. I don't think he realized that if you had a license, you had to give all the financial information to the Federal Communications Commission. At first when someone reported to me that all Gene's stock had been put up and hocked, I said, it can't be because it's never been reported. That's a violation of the FCC act. We could lose the station over it.

70

He said, you better check into it.

Sure enough it was. Security Savings I think or one of them in Los Angeles. He'd used the stock as collateral for a loan and had never reported it. So I went to Walter Bimson again and I said, I need some money and I told him what had happened.

He said, my God.

I said, I'm going to try to get Gene over here to see if we can't get this straightened out. In the meantime Del Webb had filed against us trying to get our TV license awarded to him. One of the things that would of mitigated against us terribly was the fact that Gene had hocked that station without any report to me or the FCC or anybody.

So I went to Mr. Bimson and I've forgotten how much we borrowed, a couple million dollars maybe. Anyway, I got the money and paid Gene off and got the stock and got it straightened out. And then we went to the license fight with Webb and Harry Rosenzweig. In those days, one of the principal reasons for granting a license to a station was local ownership. It was a good rule, and they leaned heavily on that. If they'd have foreclosed, any minute, Gene was in default on the loan. He lost some hotels, they were losing a lot of money. He had bought the Mark Hopkins in San Francisco. The Continental on the Strip. Several hotels. And they were really hurting. He needed a lot of money.

Eventually, we saved it and we were all right. But Webb and them, they tried very hard to take it over. And thanks to

Gene Pulliam and the paper and the people of this community, they jumped all over those guys for trying to take the station. It was a dirty, lousy thing to do. And the public really raised hell with them. All the community here was wonderful. They just jumped up in arms over it.

◆

(Editor's Note: Here are more memories of close associates of Mr. C.)

Homer Lane (associated with Chauncey in broadcasting for more than thirty years, finally as general manager and executive vice president of KOOL-AM-FM-TV): Tom always, especially in those early years, had a finger in everything, even to repairing equipment because of his expertise as a jeweler. I remember we had something go wrong with a lens and he was actually there with jeweler's rouge grinding the lens for a piece of equipment back in the shop. He was hands-on even to the point of doing things like that. Of course, entertaining clients and so forth. But with his radio background, having run KPHO, and his close association with Charlie Garland, he wasn't a novice. He understood the business.

When we were independent, we bought a lot of feature films, Laurel and Hardy stuff and that sort of thing. There were program suppliers in those days, ZIV was a big supplier of half-hour syndicated programming. But for the most part it was theatrical films. There were no off-network reruns. Video tape hadn't been invented yet and kinescope recordings were pretty bad. We had 35mm film capability. I can't remember the 35mm film projectors ever being used. It was all 16mm. And of course, everything was black and white.

We had a staff of maybe thirty, thirty-five people and we were on one floor of a two-story building, fifty feet wide by 140 feet deep at 511 West Adams, and the previous tenant of the building was Sears Roebuck where they marketed an automobile that they called the Allstate. If you remember, that was a Kaiser product and it was the Henry J. with a Sears name. The building had been empty a couple of years. We rented it and later bought it, and then piece by piece bought that whole block.

We were a great believer in advertising. We were in the advertising business. We sort of pioneered the advertising of television in newspapers. In those days the newspaper wouldn't even print our program schedule. They refused to recognize that there was such a thing as television. So in order to get our schedule published, we had to buy space to publish our schedule in the daily papers, the *Arizona Republic* and the *Phoenix Gazette*. We became their largest media advertiser, we spent more money with them than any other station or any theater or any entertainment medium. Certainly more money than any of our competitors. We were a competitor, of course. But we bought a lot of space in the newspaper and that certainly contributed. We also bought billboards.

We had a sales staff, of course. In the earlier days, a high percentage of our business was done directly with clients, rather than with advertising agencies. In later years, you very seldom dealt directly with a client, you dealt most often with advertising agencies. And we had an aggressive sales staff that just made cold calls and it was a tough sell because it wasn't just selling advertising on Channel 10, it was selling the concept of advertising on television. At the time, not every home had a television set, although it was rapidly getting into every home. It was a business that moved very, very fast. But we just called on people and called on retailers and certainly called on the big institutional advertisers, the banks and the utilities and so forth. In fact, the banks, and the major companies in town, which were the banks really, were pioneers in advertising.

For a long time, a major part of our advertising income came from automobile dealers. I remember way early on, you might remember the name Clark Smith. Clark Smith was the largest used car dealer in the state. He had several used car operations and later he developed a thing called the Clark Smith Security Plan. He was offering something like 5 or 6 percent interest on money and everybody thought that was absolutely crazy and obviously he was going to go broke. Nobody could pay that much interest. But he was an advertiser as were a good number of the used and new car dealers in town.

Of course, there are all kinds of funny stories. Everything was live in those days. We would just shoot a camera out the back door into the alley and drive cars past and hose them down first because they'd look better with the lights on them

72

and wet. Gosh, we had cars stall on camera and they had to get pushed off by hand. All sorts of things.

In the days of live television, before tape, we did our commercials live. There were a lot of funny errors made. A lot of pretty silly things happened. But those were a lot of fun days, too. The building of any new industry, any new business, is fun. Later, of course, the dollars got so big, a lot of the fun went out of it. If you made a mistake it was just so costly.

Broadcasting first of all was and is a business and a lot of people seem to forget that. They look on it almost as if it were a utility. Well, it isn't. It's a business. And it's a business that exists on advertising and if you stop to think about that for a minute, if you took television advertising out of our economy, where would our economy be? It is truly a spark plug to the economy of the country. So you're in business, you're in advertising, and you're in show business. That's the heritage of broadcasting, show business.

Later we became journalists and what in the world is more important than keeping people informed of what goes on in their community and their world? And 80 percent or so of the people look to broadcast as their prime source, not only source, but prime source of news. So that's a responsibility and with it all, you're also in a business where you can truly make a difference. How many other businesses can you think of that have all of these things wrapped up in one? There aren't any. Nothing competes.

I stumbled into the business, then wound up as a general manager of the best station in Phoenix. The most popular, the most profitable. Just the best. Obviously, no one person makes it the best but it starts at the top. That's where it all starts. It starts with the guy. And the guy was Tom.

◆

I can remember times when we both spent as many as forty hours straight without ever leaving the place, because we had problems to be solved, because we had things to do. Back in the days when competitors were trying to get our CBS affiliation agreement changed from our station to theirs, or when a group of people decided that they were going to challenge our license and put us out of business. The CBS attempt was during the 1960s. And we worked as long as forty hours at a stretch without leaving the office. But it was a labor of love, really. So, although we worked our tails off, it almost didn't even seem like work. We were just doing what we wanted to do.

We had the first video tape machine. Going way back, we were the first station on South Mountain; we built the road to the top. We were the first station to have color. We were the first station to really take news seriously. When we went on the air, we had a five or ten minute newscast sponsored by Holsum Bread, I think. A fellow named Rex Stanley did the first newscast on our station. All he did, of course, was read wire copy in front of the camera. We called that a newscast.

74

When we finally put on a regular daily newscast it was five minutes of news, five minutes of weather, five minutes of sports, five days a week and we did that twice a day at 10 p.m. and again in the early evening in conjunction with the CBS news.

Then we hired Ralph Painter from Channel 5 and we put in a Houston Fearless processor, which is a commercial-type 16mm film processor. And later we put in the first color film processor in the state, I think, for motion picture films. In fact, we had a security clearance to do work for the Department of Defense to develop their film for them.

And we were the first station to put women on the air and in key positions. In fact, our station, long before there was such a thing as EEOC, we had a woman vice-president of our company; she was our comptroller. When I came to work in 1951 we had a female Hispanic DJ. Her name at the time was Grace Gill. She later became Graciala Oliveras. First woman I think to graduate from Harvard Law, afterwards became a civil rights activist and I think she may still be.

We hired a fellow way back in the 1950s, Carlos Montaño, who was Hispanic, and he was our radio station manager. When I moved up to assistant general manager of the company, we needed someone to replace me and hired Carlos Montaño. But there just were no Hispanics in those kinds of jobs in those days in Phoenix, Arizona. And then we put Jody Knowl on the air. First female doing news. Of course, much later we had Mary Jo West as a major weekday anchor on a major newscast.

I'm talking way back when we really didn't have much of a news department. We had two people in it. We had a fellow named Jack Ware and Ralph Painter and that was the whole news department. Jack and Ralph would go out and shoot film and come back and process it and Jack would write copy to go with it and go on the air and read the copy over the film. It wasn't even sound film, it was just all silent black and white film. Then later we put the first black man on the air, a fellow by the name of Chance Williams.

Chance Williams was a journalism instructor at the University of Arizona and he called us and he said, you know, I graduated from school and I got my degree and I started teaching and I've never worked in the field and I don't know a thing about this broadcast business and I'd like to come up and work some summer for you. So we had him come up and he worked for us that summer and then he went back to the U of A and he was back there a couple of months and he called us and he said, I can't stand it. I've got to get back into it. He went to work for us full time. He came back and one of the networks, I can't remember, it was either CBS or NBC, hired him away. We trained an awful lot of people for networks.

Then we had the first Oriental on the air, a man named Sam Chu Lin. Sam Chu Lin was hired by one of the networks away from us. And we trained a lot of people who later went on to stations in Los Angeles, New York and Chicago. I'm talking about minority people, really. We trained a lot of minority people. Back in the days before it was the thing to do, Channel 10 was doing it. I remember sitting years ago in a National Association of Broadcasters meeting. I don't remember what city, it was either Washington or Chicago, listening to a Hispanic man named Richard Valenzuela who was the head of the EEOC in Arizona and he was telling people that it could be done, that they could have Hispanics and they could have a black person and they could have women on the air.

He said, if you don't know how to do it, just go out to Phoenix, Arizona and ask Channel 10 how it's done. They'll tell

75

you. Boy, that made me feel good. We hadn't made a conscious effort, gee, we've got to hire minority. We just did. And we wound up with a great staff of people.

Our first documentary was "Face of the Inner City," I think was the name of it. And that documentary actually resulted in the establishment of the LEAP program, which later took on a big name and is now the Department of Human Resources of the city. Milt Graham was mayor at the time we did this program and it got people thinking about that area south of the tracks and south of the Salt River and the mayor wanted to do something about it and Tom Chauncey and Herman Chanen put up the seed money to form the first LEAP commission. That's how that got started through our documentaries.

76

♦

When KOY decided to sell and KOOL decided to buy, we were an independent station and then became the ABC station for a short period of time. Then when Channel 3 went on the air and we were assured of getting CBS when their contract with Channel 5 ran out, we gave up ABC and Channel 3 went on the air as the ABC station. Then we went back to being an independent station for a short time before we became CBS in June of 1955, which was the big turning point for us because that's when we knew we were going to make it. Up until that time, boy!

The first TV station on the air in the Phoenix area was Channel 5 and the second station was Channel 12, which was at the time KTYL, which was over between Tempe and Mesa at Red Harkin's drive-in movie. And it was the Mesa television station. Then we were the next television station on the air and then Channel 3 came on after that. Channel 12 was on the air just months before we were, then Channel 3 came on the air a year or two after we did.

Looking back on all this, I realize that in all the years I worked with him, Tom Chauncey never second-guessed me.

♦

Tom Chauncey: That's right. You just don't do that when you put a man out front. If he made a mistake it was his mistake and I never said a word about it. He was doing what he thought was best and you don't second-guess people. You trust them. There was no reason to second-guess Homer Lane. He was an excellent man. He probably made less mistakes than I made. Why would I second-guess him? Absolutely not. He's a great man. And his wife is a great lady. They're good people. I think thirty-seven years I've known him. That's a long time. Even if I thought it was a terrible mistake I never said a word. He was smart enough to pull himself out of it if he did. He didn't make many. He was very bright. And he's honest as the day is long. Good human being.

◆

Bill Close (dean of Arizona newscasters, with Chauncey eighteen years, finally as vice-president of the news division of KOOL-AM-FM-TV): I had heard Tom had quite a temper. So when I went to KOOL, I asked very emphatically for a contract, to which he said, swell. My reasoning at that time was Tom, I know you're Irish and I've heard you have a temper, and I'd like to be able to protect myself. And he says, no problem at all.

So I had my attorney, who is now a Superior Court judge, draw up a contract. Tom just wiped it all out and put together a new contract. You know how your lawyer will do things in your favor? Well, this was 100 percent in my favor so Tom was quick to see that and rewrote a contract that was fairer. It was for two years and every once in a while, for the rest of the 16 years that I worked for Tom, he would ask, Bill, you want a new contract? Want your contract renewed?

Of course what I quickly discovered was that I didn't need any contract. He never lost his temper with me.

He had his own ideas on what was lavish and what was necessary and what you could get along without or what it'd be nice to have. If you could convince him that it was good, that it was necessary, there was no problem no matter what the cost was, within reason. At one time we had more HL76s, Ikegami cameras — we had ten or eleven of them, and CBS didn't have that many.

We had the first all color newscast on the air. In Arizona. Right here. We did it. It was said that it couldn't be done. We had one color tape machine and we shot the newscasts live in color, the editorial and sports and weather were all pre-taped.

There was a breaking story at city hall that day, so we sent one of the photographers down with a 35mm camera and shot a bunch of slides. I mean, click, click, click. We had a fellow here by the name of Jon Francken who ran our processing machine. He'd been on the Bataan death march. He got the seven chemicals in little bottles and lined them up and developed and processed that film and we had that story on the air, all in color, with slides. Wham, wham, wham. That night.

Tom would be in his office very early, six o'clock, sometimes before. He'd walk around every once in a while, walk through the news department, say hi to everyone. There was a pile of papers on Bill Lester's desk one time. Tom liked a clean desk so he used to kid Bill about getting that pile of papers out of sight. One morning, they were still there so he just pushed them all off on to the floor. He did that to Jack Murphy, only differently — he set fire to the papers. Jack got up and walked away. Tom walked the other way and somebody else put out the fire.

He liked things neat and clean. Everything in its place and a place for everything and your desk clean when you left.

78

♦

Marge Injasoulian: (with KOOL-AM-FM-TV for twenty years, ten as a promotion director, ten as vice-president for information services): Homer hired me when Tom Chauncey was out of town. I met him about a week later and I knew from that moment on that Tom Chauncey and I were going to get along just wonderfully well and be good friends, and that he was going to be a good boss and he knew I'd be a damn good employee.

I had prepared, the week he was gone, a newspaper campaign. I presented the entire campaign. I did all the layouts, my own artwork and worked up my budget.

Homer took me to him and said, Mr. Chauncey, I'd like you to meet Marge Injasoulian, our new promotion director.

He stood up and we shook hands and he said, you got something for me to see?

I laid out the whole campaign for him and he looked at it from one end to the other and said, how much is this going to cost? I told him and he looked at me and he said, it's about time. We finally have a promotion manager that knows what she's doing. He said, you have my total approval on this. Go with it. From that moment on I knew that he and I were going to be very close.

Tom Chauncey was not only a respected jeweler around the country, but he was also one of the most respected broadcasters. Again, because of his honesty and because of the quality of the programming on his station. KOOL television always was a pioneer. Always took that first step. That daringness. That risk. He was always willing to let the people do that. Let   **79** the creative people that were working with him take that risk. If they came to him with an idea, or if he had an idea, he was always willing to allow people to take that first step, that first risk.

For example, we did documentaries. We dealt with the subject of illegitimacy long before anybody would even touch it. We dealt with illegitimacy during the days when the *Arizona Republic* wouldn't accept an ad from me that had that word in the title. The program was "Illegitimacy, the Sudden Fact of Life." And the problems that we were dealing with were pregnant women, girls, unmarried pregnant women, teenagers, and the problems in our community with that. We were trying to bring that information to the public. Nobody else had done it.

We did programs on drugs. We were the first station that did anything on LSD. A gentleman took a trip on LSD and we filmed the whole thing. It was a remarkable program.

"Face of the Inner City" was another documentary that dealt with the poor in South Phoenix. No television station had ever been to South Phoenix before to cover the dilapidated homes, the condition that those people were living in down there. We did, because Tom Chauncey wanted this to be a better community for people, all people.

Tom Chauncey was never motivated by how much money the station made. Because of that quality kind of person that he was and the quality kind of programming, the city and the state are a lot better off today.

◆

Homer Lane: Many broadcasters are known in the business for doing a lot of rate cutting. We didn't do that.

In the early days of both radio and television, every station had two rate cards. They had a rate card for what they called national clients and they had a rate card for what they called local clients, and we were the first station in our market, or probably any market our size, to go to a single rate for both local and national. We got a lot of criticism from our competitors for it. But we went to a single rate and we just felt that we didn't want to be in a position where the Ford dealer and the Chevy dealer could start comparing notes and find that one was paying less than the other.

Our rate card was inviolate. Now, too, we had a wide range of advertising plans, but they were on the card and the card was available for anybody to look at whether they were the Ford Motor Company in Detroit or the Yellow Front Stores in Phoenix, Arizona, or whatever.

We were also criticized from time to time by our competitors because we were the leading station, we did have the biggest audience, and we sort of set the rate. Our philosophy was not to price ourselves out of the local market. We truly felt that it was important that the local merchant be able to afford Channel 10. And we priced ourselves accordingly so that we were affordable. As I said, we did get flack from our competitors because we were the bellwether.

We were the leader in over-all audience. We were the leader in news audience. You stop to think about the television business, especially you take the three networks, now everyone makes a big thing about which network is first, second and third. But if you look at the numbers, there's not a heck of a lot of difference between first and third. They're all pretty close. And one network may be the leader this year and CBS I guess is third place this year. Well, for years they were first place. In the different markets at any given time you'll find the Number One station to be the ABC or the CBS or the NBC station.

So what's the difference? Well, the difference of course is what you do locally. And what people do locally, really, is their news operation. We recognized that very early and we poured big hunks of our resources into news considerably before it was the universal thing to do. So we got kind of a jump on the other stations in that respect I guess, and we were always forging ahead, trying to stay ahead.

The big difference between television in those days and today, I think, is one of economics. In this respect, the entrepreneurs, the people that built the stations are gone, pretty much. And most stations now are owned by public companies, and the objective of any public company is necessarily different from the objective of a little closely held deal with three or four stockholders, or a family, or a person. And we had the distinct advantage of not having debt because we built the place. We didn't buy it, we built it.   **81**

We were able to decide that we were going to have the best news operation regardless of what it took. No public company can do that because that's not the way our system works. There is only one objective for any public company and that's adequate return for the stockholder and improving it year to year or quarter to quarter, month to month, whatever unit of measure, so that everybody's job depends on improving. And you get a whole different perspective on what you're going to do and how you're going to do it.

We had the luxury of being a very small company, we had just three stockholders in the later years, Gene Autry, Tom Chauncey and me.

We also had very sizable Christmas bonuses, for those of us in executive positions and department heads and long-time employees, all the way down to the newest two-week old employee would get something. If they'd been there two weeks, they'd at least get twenty-five dollars or something. Always. But we had bonuses that would go as high as 50 percent of a year's salary. And we established a profit-sharing plan in 1960. When we were running the profit-sharing plan before we had to turn it over to one of the banks, we made a lot more money than the bank ever did with it. We were investing in our own business, and we did very well with it. Made a lot of money with it for the employees.

I hate to use the word "employees" because we really had an organization of 200 people that operated more like a family than like a business organization or a corporation. True, we were technically a corporation because we were incorporated. But it was operated just as a bunch of friends with Tom as the head of the family. That's just the way it was. We had the greatest staff in the history of the business. We brought together some great, great people. Some great, great talents who all worked together and it was the only organization of anywhere near its size that I had ever come in contact with that had almost no office jealousies, no office politics. They just didn't exist in that organization.

Tom Chauncey certainly was one of the people who gave to the broadcasting business a conscience and the broadcasting business did have a conscience. Perhaps still has in some areas. It's rapidly becoming a thing of the past as more and more of the stations, the entrepreneurs die, retire, sell. The public companies operate them as investments, as cash cows. And that conscience is gradually diminishing. We did not operate Channel 10 to make the most money we could make. We wanted to be solvent, of course. We wanted to make money, of course. We wanted to live well, drive nice automobiles, of course. But not to the exclusion of actually serving our community. That philosophy comes in any broadcast operation or any business from a person. And for Channel 10 that person was Tom.

Being in broadcasting in Phoenix was a great ride, let me tell you. It was just a thrill a minute. It was my life and his life. It was so much more than a business. So much more. It was a life and we really felt we were doing some good. And we did a lot of good. We did so many things for the community.

◆

Bill Miller (started with KOOL-TV in the lowest entry position on a floor crew, after twenty years was manager of its news division, went on to become vice-president and station manager of KTVK-Channel 3): I started in 1962 on the floor crew and Maurie Helle and I would dream of producing television programs, which is a big dream for a couple of kids working on the floor crew. The biggest show in the country at that time was "Hootenanny" on the ABC Television Network, and we thought, well that would be something that we could do. So we got permission to do a pilot show with folk music. We got folk singers from some little coffee houses in Scottsdale and we produced a half-hour pilot and took it in and we showed it to Mr. Chauncey. Four or five executives would sit around and he would be thinking and thinking and they would all be looking at him trying to decide what their opinion of this was going to be.

Then he said, I really like this show. What do you have in mind? Well, we were thinking of doing this maybe once a month on a Saturday night, maybe for an hour. He said, no, no. Let's do it every day.

Every day?

Yeah, every day.

So we did. We ran it every afternoon I think from four to four-thirty, just before the "Mickey Mouse Club," every day for months, hundreds of episodes. We stayed on the floor crew, both Helle and I, and I think we were paid six hours of overtime a week to produce this show. But it was an incredible opportunity. Later we said, we really ought to think about doing a documentary because they're giving Emmys for documentaries. We had never done a documentary before in our life. We went to see Mr. Chauncey and said, you know, you liked this other show so well, why don't you let us do a documentary on the inner city?

We didn't realize that the inner city was his pet project at the moment. I think it was happenstance. That documentary was called "Face of the Inner City." It started out to be an hour but I think it ended up being more like seventy-five minutes.

We received a lot of public attention off of that show because people didn't do local documentaries in those days and it was the first time the people of Phoenix looked at their city on television and said, my God, we've got some real problems in this town. We've got some sad situations, and some terrible housing. They just never realized it was there before. And the program and the efforts of Mr. Chauncey and others, were really the basis for what then became Operation LEAP, and I guess it's now the Human Resources department of the city of Phoenix.

When that happened, we shifted our interest. We continued to do some of these entertainment kind of programs, but we shifted our interests into documentaries and again, Mr.

83

Chauncey at this point had a vision that there would be community interest in local documentaries and with them he could really help the community and so we started doing local documentaries on a regular basis. By the time he left the station, we had done maybe fifty-six local specials in twelve months. That's how big they had become.

We had a staff of nine or ten doing special projects. It was just incredible. And we all learned a lot. It was good for the station. I think it was terribly good for the community, and those programs still show today in schools. Unfortunately, most of the time they lost money. I don't think we ever made any money on special programs — but we did help build a special image for the station.

84

◆

KOOL didn't operate the same way that a corporate television station operates today. We didn't have budgets, for instance. We didn't have the same kind of business. And I didn't know about those things. Here I was the news director at one of the most successful CBS affiliates in the country and I really didn't know anything about budgets. I really didn't know anything about economic planning.

When the new owners came in, I had to learn fast.

◆

Tom Chauncey: And then there came a day when some folks came in and said, we're going to buy you out. Oh. That was the worst day of my life. They didn't come and ask me, they told me. They told me they were going to buy me and they said they'd bury me. Period.

We were just too successful. Everybody was after us. It had been going on for years. These people came in and just flat told me that one way or the other they'd get the station. Period. I don't know how much they could do that in these times, but they did. And after a fortune in legal fees, Frank Snell said to me, Tom, it's going to kill you, you've had open heart surgery. You're a friend, I know you don't want to give it up, but you better give it up because you'll be ten years fighting these people.

And they played dirty games. They boasted they'd kill me one way or the other, because I'd had open heart surgery and they would end up with my station out of my estate or something. They made no bones about it. I think it's the worst thing that ever happened to this country, that those kinds of people. . . .

They didn't have it very long. They didn't want it to serve this community, no public necessity, convenience, nothing. What they did was they used it to sell a bunch of other stations that they owned. And it wasn't very long before they sold it all for a fortune. In a year's time, they had to make over $100,000,000 clear.

◆

In the early days of television you saw everybody at the network. I was in New York a lot and we were all pioneers.

Ed Murrow became better liked after he died. Murrow was kind of stuffy, but he was great, and a lot of the guys, they respected his ability. The greatest thing about Edward R. Murrow was his voice and timing. He was good and he had guts.

I met Walter Cronkite when he came to the network. We were a small family then. You had Mr. William Paley, then came Dr. Frank Stanton. Dr. Stanton was a teacher, a very brilliant man, obviously. And Jack Van Valkenberg was one of our first presidents. I worked with every one of them. And all the vice-presidents of programming, all of them. We had a lot of input in those days.

We were very close, the heads of programming and all. Fortunately, I had a lot of opportunity to express my opinions and make suggestions such as more news.

I was chairman of the affiliates board and I met Richard S. Salant, president of the news. I met him once in Tucson and at that time we only had a fifteen-minute newscast, which meant ten or twelve minutes of news, the rest was commercials. Well, you couldn't do much news in ten minutes. They had tried several times a half-hour news, which would be a lot better, but the affiliates kept turning it down. I met him at a hamburger joint and I said, Dick, why don't you just do it?

He said, what do you mean, just do it?

Who's going to turn it down? Why don't you just say we're going to have a half-hour news come a certain time?

Would you go for that?

I absolutely would. And I would even tell them that I suggested it. But if you keep balloting and messing around getting permission, we'll never have a half-hour news. Let's just do it. Set a date and do it, and the screams will all go up and if they want to run me off the board OK, but let's just do it. Let's take a half-hour news and do it.

Fine. If you can live with it, we can.

That's how we got a half-hour news. But it took two or three years getting it done.

Later, that same kind of situation came up with "60 Minutes." It wasn't running in prime time and it wasn't doing very well, either. So I just told Dick Salant, go ahead and move it into prime time, just announce the schedule and don't take any more votes on it. So he did and look how well "60 Minutes" has done.

Of anything, I think those are the best things I accomplished in broadcasting. Those and getting section 315 changed, which was to allow the Nixon-Kennedy debates. I was very active in that with Dr. Stanton.

We wanted to do the Nixon-Kennedy debates and I spent lots of time in Washington. It finally got passed. Dr. Stanton was really tremendous. We spent lots of time together. That's 1960.

The primary people were Mr. Paley and Dr. Stanton, Dick Salant, all the people at the network of course, and Senator Hayden and the head of the Communications and Commerce committee, which included television. There were quite a few of us. It was terribly hard to get agreement for it. Kennedy wanted it.

Vice President Nixon certainly didn't want it. He knew how much charisma Kennedy had, a lot of charisma. Nixon wasn't too anxious to do it. A lot of Congressmen didn't want to do it. A lot of Senators. It was at the leading edge of something that had never been done. Never permitted, and we got in lots of fights. I appeared before committees, as did Dr. Stanton, of course, he was there every week. But we'd gone almost up to the wire and thought we weren't even going to get it done then. We finally got it done in time to have the Kennedy-Nixon debates.

But you know, we probably wouldn't have succeeded if it hadn't been for Joe Duke, the sergeant-at-arms of the U.S. Senate. I've known Joe Duke so long I don't know where I first met him. We're very close friends and have been a very long time. I'd guess he got his job through Senator Hayden. Joe just loved Senator Hayden. He just adored the man. And Joe was a hard worker. I think probably the person who had the most power in the senate was Joe Duke. He assigned all the offices. He assigned the cars. And they all liked him because he was a very nice man.

He helped me by introducing me to people. I could get in any place in two minutes. Absolutely. Every door was open if you knew Joe Duke. No matter what came up. I would be in the office of the Speaker of the House. I would be in the Minority Leader's office. I was every place. And they were opened immediately. And they would know I was a friend of Senator Hayden's.

Just go in and tell them this country wasn't free, that it would never be free until broadcasting had the same rights as the newspapers. The voters would not know what the candidates were like unless they had debates. And we also told them that sometimes people of our own political persuasion, our own beliefs were going to be defeated since they wouldn't debate as well. But that's the way it started and that's important, that this medium was a second-class citizen until we could have debates.

Nobody in the world in their right mind would want to debate John Fitzgerald Kennedy. Nobody. I assure you that Vice President Nixon did not want to debate. Look at the publicity you give the other man. You put him right out in front. And this is the biggest argument we had with all the Senate. We just had a hell of a time. But we worked hard at it and Dr. Stanton was beautiful. CBS had a corporate executive by the name of E. Kidder Mead who was a brilliant man. CBS also had a man by the name of Ed Bunker who was head of the affiliates. That was the team that pretty much worked together. In those days we got to know every administrative assistant to all the Senators and Congressmen. As far as broadcasting, that and news, if I made a contribution as a pioneer, that was it. Jack Kennedy of course elected himself but the debates had a tremendous impact.

I have two gifts in there from CBS they sent me after it was over with. They're very valuable. One's a big blunderbuss, a handmade gun, from back in the time of our first colonies. Freedom. The other piece is a wooden Indian standing, a cigar store Indian. It's a very lovely piece.

♦

I believe the day will come when they'll have a whole hour of news three or more times a day on the network, and they should. They should have a morning, noon, 6 and 10 or 11 o'clock news. They have the facilities, they have the people and there's the appetite for it and they will never be first-class without it.

The trouble now with news is that the limited time means that they do mostly hard news and they're the bearer of bad tidings most of the time. If they had more time, they could be the bearer of some good tidings, too. They really should have four regularly-scheduled hourly newscasts a day. And I predict the network that will do it will be the leader. And one of them will have the guts to do it some day. I recommended it and I certainly would recommend it if I were there. I won't be active again in broadcasting, but I think it's very important. Actually, it would help the newspapers because after what TV would show them, the people would go seek out the rest of the story.

♦

For some reason or other, I decided I wanted our stations, both radio and television, to be the very best in news. News would be the thing.

Why I decided that, I really don't know. It may be because having only finished the eighth grade, I myself wanted to learn more about history and geography and what goes on in the community and state. I was curious like most kids. I think you become a little less curious as you get older — not much, though. Really, a kid's nosy.

Or maybe it was being across the street from the *Republic* and *Gazette,* watching men like Charlie Stauffer and Wes Knorpp and Gene Pulliam and all those people and journalists, Reg Manning and some great newspaper people. I knew them on a day-to-day basis.

News fascinated me. It was the thing I thought broadcasting could do best. I don't think you do a good job with a license unless you do have a good news department. I think you need to do it. That doesn't mean you have to lose money at it, either. It was very costly. In the beginning, particularly, we spent a lot of money. We probably did more documentaries than anybody else in the country. And that's unheard of for a private station. It was privately owned and we had no money source other than what we could generate. But we had a separate documentary department. That's all they did. We really had a group of people who were fantastic. Young, dedicated people. We had the largest staff of newspeople in the state, electronically. When I left, we probably had about eighty working with news.

Even so, we made money. We made a lot of money. We had to make money to keep doing it. That doesn't mean you have to waste it.

I would call the newspeople in and say, you're going to do X number of stories a day. And I think that's basic to the business. That's what they're there for, to put something on the air. But all of a sudden you'd get some of these people —news journalists — who think if they do something once a month, that's fine. That might be fine for them, but that doesn't pay the bills.

I used to tell our people to look in the mirror every morning and just say to themselves, I ain't that good. I'd say, I don't mean to admonish you, but when you're shaving in the morning say to yourself, I ain't that good. Or when you're making up, to the gals. We always had a lot of gals on the air. I said, I won't bother you, but if I ever catch you being deceitful or setting up a story, there won't be any meeting. You'll be fired. I won't tolerate unfair journalism.

And I did have to fire a few who didn't believe me. But after a few it wasn't very hard. I never asked them to berate themselves. I never asked them to do anything unfair. I asked them to be fair. I had people there a long time. Homer Lane was with me thirty-some years.

89

We were the only station in the country to do editorials on a day-to-day basis for years. The only station in the country that had a separate documentary department and Homer and I looked at every one of those before it went on the air to be sure they were balanced and honest.

We'd ask questions. The creative people would say, you have no right to do that. Well, I think you have a right if you're paying the bills. It's my license, my partner's license, and I say that when I get that license, that I will be fair. Broadcasting, journalism, news people must be free. Must be absolutely free and unfettered, but they must be fair. If they're not fair and responsible, they don't deserve to have the license and they don't deserve to tell the story.

We had some very talented people. They're now all over the country, ones who trained with us who have become very good journalists. They were all seeking fame and fortune, 99 percent of them of course wanted to go to New York on the network. And many did.

♦

With deregulation now, it's tougher, but it's better. The only thing that was intended in the beginning, back in the 1920s with the original Hoover act licensing radio stations, was to regulate radio like traffic, the streets. To keep your car from going in all directions, to keep the radio stations from bumping into each other, the licensing was to keep signals from bumping into each other. It was never intended to interfere with programming.

The government has no business in programming. Programming is none of their damn business, unless it's dishonest. The government and Congress, what would they want? They want to look good, don't they? If they had their way they'd tell you they want you to make them look good. That's not good journalism. I've had politicians call up and say, we want you to do this story or that one to make them look good. But no, we don't do that. Some stations have, some have kowtowed to them. But a good station does one thing — it tells the truth and it tells it fairly. Whether it's radio or television, you don't let your news staff run all over you. You don't let them abuse people. You don't have a license to steal. You don't have a license to abuse. You don't have a license to corrupt.

I think if you run a news department and you're the head of it, you have to say to yourself first, is this respectful? Do I respect these people, our citizens who are our audience? Do I care about humanity? And that isn't just the rich. I'm talking about the poor, the hungry, the maimed. Are they being treated respectfully? Is it in good taste? And are we getting the whole story and both sides of it, if there are both sides? And that's what we fought for so hard and that's where Homer Lane was a godsend, because if I were out of town or something, he knew damn well the things that I wouldn't tolerate. And sometimes he was harder to get by than me because he knew, and I'm sure that over the years Homer disagreed with a lot of things I scotched, but he had a hell of a mind on him. But I would not permit something on there that I thought was degrading to people.

91

News is a great thing if it's handled right. News must be absolutely free and unfettered of the boss. But with that freedom comes a great responsibility on the reporter. If they aren't careful, bad practices create bad laws. And the worst thing that could happen to this country is to have the government tell you what you can or cannot put on the air in news. The government has no business in programming. It was never intended to be there — or in the news.

A Congressman has no business calling up and saying, you can't put this or that on the air — but they did it constantly. We just said no. It's a story. It stands. You can't blame them. They don't want to look bad. But usually when they called you knew that the story was true. They were trying to stop it. A lot of people called me. Arizona people and others. They knew I was highly connected in Washington, New York. A lot of people called me.

◆

I believe that the newscasters have no right to sacrifice people's reputations the way some of them do, no business going into their closets and back doors. Jesse Jackson said, somebody asked him a question about the press and he said, if I'm

President, when I go on the second floor and close the door, that's my business. And that's true.

The press, in the old days, they'd never talk about a lot of people the way they have been doing lately. Those things are not to be talked about. A lot of people have problems, If a star has a personal problem, that doesn't affect all of America, you know.

You don't have a witch-hunting license when you have a license on the air. Television is so strong, you can crucify people. And I wouldn't tolerate it.

I've had on-the-air people say to me, you can't censor me. And I said, no, but I can fire you. I'm telling you the policy is simple: Fairness.

In the early days, station owners had a lot of input with the networks. We looked at shows. We fought over shows. We had a lot to do with program practices. We had one thing in common, everybody that was in the network early on and was active in the network: leave the news department alone. Don't go in there and nitpick, but give them rules and practices. Make them get the story and cover both sides of the story and be honest. Don't cheat. But then leave it alone.

And I have sat in Dr. Stanton's office and Mr. Paley's office when President after President called and screamed his head off. Presidents of the United States. Senators. Congressmen.

They'd say, you can't run that story.

And Stanton, Paley would answer, sorry, we do not interfere. If you can tell me that it's a dishonest story or that it's wrong or that we're not being fair to you, I will look into it. But we do not interfere with the news department.

Never did. Never. Lyndon Johnson, you could hear him banging on the phone from the White House. Just screaming his head off. Putting him in a bad light, he thought. But the network never changed the story. They were steadfast in the support of the newsmen.

◆

The 1968 Democratic party convention in Chicago, do you remember what a fiasco? It was so horrible. It was so horrible and a lot of the affiliates and owners were on top of the network, screaming their heads off about the coverage being slanted and unfair. Luckily in Phoenix we had just gotten a couple of the big, huge tape machines, the heavy tapes, the Ampexes. And they were huge and cost a fortune and I talked to Dick Salant, the president of CBS news, and I said, Dick, something has got to be done. This thing is getting completely out of hand. I said, do you see any objection to getting together with a bunch of people and sitting around a room and looking at the Chicago tape by the hour?

He said, no, so I got Dr. Stanton and I told him and he said, that's a good idea. I said, I'll host it at the Biltmore in Phoenix. We have two projectors, tapes, they're mammoth, as big as that building. And we disconnected them and hauled them out there and we spent hours looking at every bit of Chicago tape to see whether it was balanced.

We had Dr. Stanton plus the owners, a majority of the owners. The news people. Walter. Everybody, 100 or so.

It lasted for hours. We looked at everything. Contrary to what the critics had been saying, the network did a good job. You know, it really did happen. You don't hide that kind of stuff. Anyway, it was worthwhile and I was awfully glad we did it. It was a tough risk because we took the videotape machines out of the studio and if something had happened to one of them, we'd have been in trouble trying to run a station. In those days, you know, with all the new stations being built, you couldn't rent one or get a spare machine. Now you could get dozens of them. But in those days it was tough. You're also not supposed to move them around like that. We just put them on a pickup and hauled them. But it worked out great and we really had quite a meeting.

The conclusions? That indeed the network news folks had done a very noble job. It was unanimous.

◆

There was a time when the most respected people in the world were television journalists. Walter Cronkite, the most respected man in television, and many thought Number One in the U.S. An extraordinary man. Easy to be around. Lovely wife. Common as an old shoe. I'm very fond of him. He was the best thing that ever happened to television.

The worst thing that ever happened to television is Sam Donaldson. You only find an arrogant son of a bitch like a Sam Donaldson every once in a while, and he is arrogant. I've never seen Walter Cronkite abuse a soul. He was Number One all the time. He never abused anybody. But he told the stories; he told the stuff, the stories, as well as anybody. And asked tough questions.

But Donaldson is combative. Somebody could have fired Donaldson a long time ago and this network news would have been a lot better. He's just plain mean. A person came up to see me once and said, I think you ought to know that I visited with Sam Donaldson's mother in New Mexico when he was a kid. He said, that mean little rascal kicked me in the shins, he was mean even as a youngster.

I think Donaldson's abruptness and all is ignorance. If you're smart enough, you don't need to be mean. You get your point across softly. I don't think he's that bright. He's just mean.

I got so riled up at Donaldson and a few others that I bought an ad in *USA Today* to protest the way they were treating President Reagan. It cost me 30,000-some dollars. I don't like to waste money but I thought it was necessary at the time, and I do feel there has been more respect shown since then.

♦

I was for a long time and still am in fear of some bad laws being passed about the press. And I think if the press continues to be unfair and not be careful about what they say and not balance the stories, there will be laws passed that will limit their ability to be free and unfettered. And if you don't have a free and unfettered press, you don't have a free America. With the Donaldsons and those kinds of people, picky, picky, picky, it would have been very easy to get Congress, I'm sure, to pass a law infringing on the rights of free press. That would be the worst thing that could happen to the United States. People were so disgusted. Nobody likes the bearer of bad tidings. Hell, they used to shoot them if they brought bad news. But they don't have to be nasty about it. They have to be fair.

Broadcasting

95

The arrogance and pomposity of some members of the Press is an embarrassment to responsible journalists everywhere. Whatever happened to the concept of respect for our President and the office he holds? Not since the revilement of President Hoover have we seen such outrageous treatment of the Institution of the Presidency by the White House Press Corps.

As a 50 year Broadcaster, I have been ashamed of the lack of professionalism exhibited by some of these people who pretend to be journalists. President Reagan is our President. He serves all the people of our great Nation, including members of the Press. He and his office have the respect of most Americans. He and his office deserve the respect of all Americans.

Tom Chauncey
Phoenix-Scottsdale, Arizona

December 1, 1986

And I was very concerned that freedom of the press was going to lose some of its rights.

The feedback from that ad was unbelievable. I didn't get any rest for a month. Nothing but phone calls wanting me to go on the air, wanting me to come here, go there. I did some of them, but I couldn't do them all. I did go on the air a few times with friends of mine that I'd known. They said, do you want to say something? And I did. It was unbelievable. People were very grateful that I did it. And a lot of station owners don't want that nasty attitude to prevail in journalism.

You keep doing these kinds of things, you open the door for a bad law. And with a bad law, which leaves us essentially without a free press, you may as well shut up the doors of America.

96

♦

As I look back on all those years in broadcasting, I suddenly realize that while we had a lot of people threaten us, we actually had fewer than a half dozen libel suits that went to trial.

We never paid off to avoid a trial.

And we never had a libel judgment entered against us.

That's not a bad record for forty years on the air. At least some of it came about because I guess I was a crank about being fair with the news — not so much because I was afraid of lawsuits but because I wanted to be sure that the news was balanced and that people respected our news as something they could believe in.

That's really the whole point of having a TV station, isn't it?

Chapter 7

Presidents of
the United States

I had a friend by the name of O. L. McDaniel who became Speaker of the Arizona House. Democrat, cattleman, rancher. One of the nicest men I ever knew, close personal friend. He said to me, Harry Truman is coming to Yuma on a train and we ought to go down there and meet him and ride back with him. He's running for President of the United States and he's a good man and we ought to go say hello to him.

We took a fellow by the name of John Babbitt, one of the senior Babbitts. And there were two or three others. So we went down and met the train. Got on the train with the President and rode to Phoenix with him, and had interviews with him, talked with him, visited with him. And I thought I was a smart-ass. I was stupid, I was flustered, I didn't have that much sense.

I was trying to think of something to say and I said, Mr. President, the Catholics are wondering where you stand. You don't seem to say very much and they don't know much about you; they don't know how you're going to react to the Catholic religion and so on. Everything they see about you, you're a Mason. And I said, I think it's going to hurt you.

He looked at me and got mad. He said, listen young man. He reached in his pocket and he pulled out a rosary and he said, look at that. Guess where that came from?

I said, what are you doing with a rosary?

He said, the Pope gave it to me and I carry it with me all the time. He said, tell your Catholic friends they can stuff it.

I said, all right, Mr. President. Hell, that's fine. Then he started laughing. But I riled him. He had it right in his pocket.

Right then and there. He said, I carry this all the time. And he was delightful. I said to McDaniel and Babbitt, both state legislators, this man needs to meet more people, that's all. If he meets more people, he'll be President. You're going to like him if you meet him. And you did like him.

Boy, did he come across in person. I'll tell you, when you walked in that room, you knew you were in the presence of a very bright, brilliant man. He could have clobbered me. I had no business saying what I did.

◆

98   President Eisenhower made me U.S. Ambassador to Nigeria for its independence ceremonies in 1960. I was a Democrat and he of course was a Republican president. And he also appointed Governor Nelson Rockefeller, and the two of us were ambassadors and representatives of President Eisenhower.

You know, they don't offer you that position until they know you'll take it. They don't want the bad press, they don't want anyone to say, well I was offered that and I turned it down. First they find out if you'll do it. So I had a call from a friend who said, you're going to get a call from the White House. Well I'm glad he told me. It would have scared the hell out of me. And they're going to ask you to be ambassador and represent the President.

I said, why? What for?

And he said, well, they're going to have the independence of Nigeria and you've been recommended very highly as one who would go in there with the black people and you know how to behave yourself, you have no prejudices. They said they believe you can handle yourself well.

I said, well I'm flattered, but I'll have to talk to my wife. And they said, oh she doesn't go. And I said, if she doesn't go, I don't go. That's a hell of a thing to say to the White House.

What are you talking about, he says. You're being offered—

And I said, listen. You're going to send me over there and you're going to have me represent the United State of America with Nelson Rockefeller and I'm supposed to go out there to all these social things. You're going to have the princes and the kings and all these people from all these great countries. Every country was represented. It was a great honor. And I said, I don't know anything about this stuff. But a woman will understand. I said, I'm just not going to go without her. I need somebody with me.

They said, we'll get back to you. So they had to go back to the President. He said, let him take her.

So then what happened, they told Nelson Rockefeller that my wife was going so he had to bring his wife. So he brought Todd even though they were about to get a divorce.

Then I really did get a call from the White House and it was Mr. Eisenhower and I said, yes, I was honored and thank you.

The next call I get is from the State Department. Will you appear on certain days for briefings? And I said, yes sir, I'll be there. So I took my wife and we spent two days at the State Department, briefings, briefings, briefings. And we're ready to take off and I didn't know I had Air Force One. I had no idea. I didn't know that the Presidents ever do that. So they said, we have to stop in New York and pick up the Rockefellers. And here, lo and behold, we've got Air Force One.

Anyways, I'm armed with all my information which was very slim. I didn't know a damn thing. I was a lost babe in the woods. Stupid. And Rockefeller got on in New York, he and Mrs. Rockefeller, Todd, and we're visiting. Talking about mutual friends.

The airplane is absolutely gorgeous, you've got all this space. A whole switchboard so the President can be in touch with anywhere in the world, a stateroom for our wives, a room each for the Governor and me, a galley, an eating place, then regular airline seats for the press and the dignitaries. It was quite a show.

The Governor said, how much do you know about where we're going? I said, nothing. We've had briefings, they've been nice but not too helpful. And he said, come with me and we went into a room and there were these people there and he said, brief Mr. Chauncey. And they had books and stuff. I'd never seen such research in my life. So in about an hour and a half I knew more about Nigeria than the Nigerians did.

Now, he said, you just watch what I do. But he would never get in front of me. He always shoved me out there. Very thoughtful. I'd say, Governor —

No, you're the lead man. I'll be right here to help you. And every place we went I'd try to lean back but it didn't work. In fact, when we landed in Lagos and they had all these officials and the bugles blew a fanfare and I was holding back and all of a sudden the Governor goosed me, but good, and then I really was out in front.

We had United States Day. This was a day where they were putting on their Sunday best and they brought all their artifacts and their artwork and the museum pieces and historical pieces and of course, all the countries were there. Princess Anne from England, everybody was there from all the countries. The Russians were there. And all representatives, high-ranking people, except me. Of course, Governor Rockefeller was pretty well-known.

And I saw this elephant table, which I now have. It was done by a kid that still had hash knife cuts in his face, you know, he was out of the bush. But the elephant was gorgeous and I loved it. It was a piece of artwork and I asked are any of these things for sale? And our escort said, I don't know, I'll find out for you. He came back and he said, they'd love to sell them. I said, I'd like to buy the elephant.

Well, my wife kicked me and said, you can't do that. This is the United States Day here and you're buying artwork in the middle of it. I said, what's the difference? They want the money. They don't have to sell it.

I asked the man, is this embarrassing? He said, no. If you want it, he wants to sell it. He wants the money. So I bought it, paid for it, only a few hundred dollars.

We each had cars, we had these big, long limousines, bullet-proofed and they had the flag of the country and our flag, and there were two U.S. security men that were assigned to us all the time around the clock. We had another reception that night and the Governor said to me, Tom, how are you going to get that table home?

They're going to send it to me.

Don't fall for that. We bought stuff over here five years ago we still don't have. Rarely do you get the things. It's lost along the way or something happens and if you really want that elephant, you better let me have my men get it for you.

I said, what are we going to do with it then?

Put it on Air Force One with us.

But I can't do that.

Yes you can. It's your airplane now. We can do that. The President wouldn't care. It's just us and our wives in this big airplane. So sure enough, he got it for me and put it on the plane.

We arrived in New York and we were invited to stay at the Rockefellers, and I'm home a few days and someone sends me a fairly good-sized picture from the *New York Times* of three men unloading an elephant off of Air Force One in New York City. And it talks about Thomas Chauncey from Phoenix, Arizona, representative of President Eisenhower and Ambassador and on and on and on. Then the bottom line, the last line says, Nelson Rockefeller also attended. God, I thought I would die. Some guy with a sense of humor. I was nobody, absolutely nothing.

◆

There was one other time I'd done some work for President Eisenhower.

I was called to Washington. A friend of mine, Robert B. Anderson, was the Secretary of the Treasury, and he and the President were very close, dear friends. He's the man that the President wanted to succeed him. He didn't want Nixon. He wanted Bob Anderson for President; Nelson Rockefeller told me on the trip President Eisenhower didn't think Nixon would make a good President.

Anyway, I landed at National airport. I had two or three friends with me. And I'd never seen such a reception. Colonels, Army, Navy, Air Force, Marines, Coast Guard. With aides. Lined up. Cars.

The last colonel said, congratulations, Mr. Chauncey. Welcome. The President would like to see you at X hours. But before that, the Secretary of the Treasury would like to see you and if you don't mind, our people will take your bags to your hotel and take your guests. The Secretary would like to see you right away.

So I went over there and Bob Anderson said, Tom, Monday the President goes before Congress. And we're getting a lot of flak about the budget. I can tell you honestly that it's a good budget. It's a reasonable budget and it's very sensible. It's just politics; they're trying to make the President look bad and they shouldn't. And we think maybe you can help. Would you talk to Senator Hayden for us before the President goes over there?

I said, sure. I don't know what the hell I'm talking about, but I'll be glad to. I know that he's always in the office at 6:30-7 a.m. and I can walk right in and I always do and I'm going to see him anyway. I'll be there tomorrow morning. And I'll go in and talk to him, but I don't know what I'm talking about.

He said, I can assure you that it's a very good budget. And we know that the Senator does his homework, he always has.

So I went in, all the greetings, you know, Tom how are you? I loved the man, he loved me. And I said, Senator, I don't know whether I should be here or not for this, but let me tell you what has happened to me. I can't believe it but — and I told him my story.

He looked at me and he said, well, I've looked at it. It's a good budget. You can tell the President that we'll okay it. It will be done Monday morning.

So help me. I went back to the hotel. That night I was invited to use his yacht Sequoia by the President. So I told my friends and they were all laughing and one very, very anti-everything guy, he didn't believe it, he was critical of everything, he said, your leg's being pulled. You're not about to get on that boat. You're just crazy. You're going to go out there and get embarrassed.

Anyway, I invited about four or five people, whoever I wanted for dinner. And this guy says, you know this is silly because you know damn well — but anyway, he came, too. And here's the military all lined up, piping you on; I didn't know

The lobby of the Adams Hotel, where I started as a page boy when I was 13. Third from the left is W.D. Chauncey, my older brother who was assistant manager of the Adams, and fourth from the right, sitting on the counter, is Jack Kane, bell captain when I started there and later the hotel's general manager. The picture probably was taken in the late 1920s, and the guys in Western garb probably were members of the Phoenix Junior Chamber of Commerce publicizing their annual rodeo.

During my
jewelry store
days.

PLEASE BRING THIS CARD WITH YOU

The Government of the Federation of Nigeria

has the honour to invite

Mr. & Mrs. T. Chauncey

to

a State Ball at the Federal Palace Hotel,

on Saturday the 1st of October, 1960, at 9 p.m.

President Eisenhower named me Special Ambassador to Nigeria for that country's Independence Day ceremonies in 1960. This is an invitation to us to attend the State Ball the government sponsored.

My office at the KOOL-AM-FM-TV station headquarters was not small. Sometimes the entire staff would meet there.

Richard Boone, Paladin of the *Have Gun, Will Travel* television series, Governor Fannin and I help open the 1959 Arizona State Fair.

Senator Carl Hayden's 50th anniversary dinner drew many of the top U.S. government officials to Phoenix. Here are President John F. Kennedy, the Senator, me, and Representative Morris "Mo" Udall. I was chairman for the event and Jimmy Minotto, half-hidden behind the president, was honorary chairman.

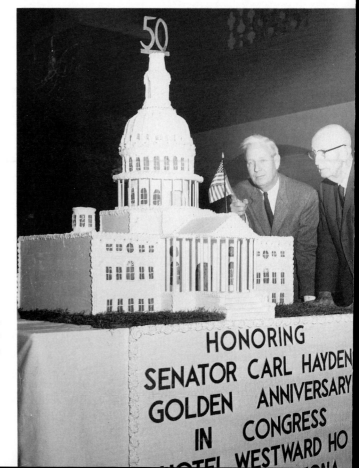

No cardboard here — that's a real cake Senator Hayden and I are admiring.

HONORING
SENATOR CARL HAYDEN
GOLDEN ANNIVERSARY
IN CONGRESS
WESTWARD HO

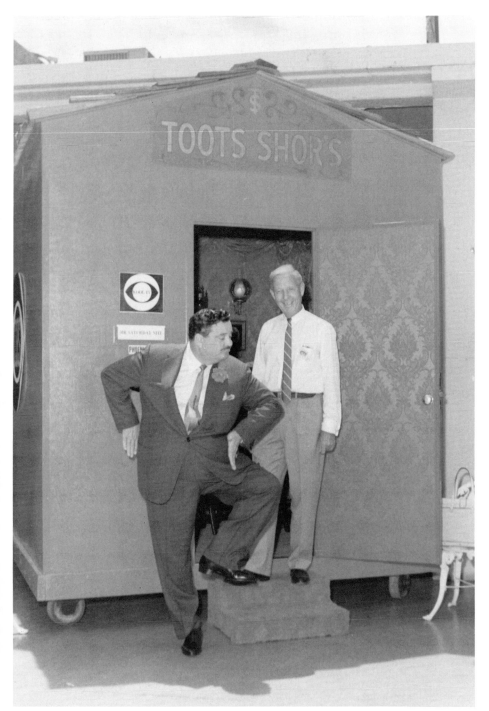

To make Jackie Gleason feel at home during a stop in Phoenix, I borrowed a Toots Shor's reproduction from a Hollywood movie set. It worked.

Broadcasting-Telecasting March 25, 1957

Both our radio and television stations dominated the Phoenix market. KOOL-TV had this tremendous lead.

When I helped Herman Chanen meet the United Fund goal for the Phoenix
area for the first time in years, Herman named an award after me — and then
gave me the first one. That's a duplicate of the real Rose Bowl.

The moment the world changed — the Arabian horse world, that is. This is right after I won the prize Arabian Naborr with a record $150,000 auction bid.

And here's a painting of Naborr by Artist Gladys Brown Edwards.

A joke from Dr. Khris Kirkland-West, veterinarian and ranch manager for Tom Chauncey Arabians, cracks me up.

Dr. Khris with T C Echo, son of Naborr, born June 25, 1976, the morning the U.S. Echo Satellite went into orbit around the world.

Here I am receiving the honorary Doctor of Humane Letters degree from Arizona State University. President Russ Nelson supervises the 1983 ceremony.

This is the horse with which I set another record — Gardenia, for which I paid $1,500,000.

(Top, right page) I like to feed carrots to the horses, especially Champion Ben Bask.

(Bottom, right page) I was made an honorary Thunderbird in 1987.

Lois and Herman Chanen
request the pleasure of your company
for a very special
SURPRISE Birthday Party
honoring our dear friend
Tom Chauncey
Monday, the nineteenth of January
Nineteen hundred and eighty-seven
six-thirty in the evening
The Arizona Biltmore
Aztec Lounge
Phoenix

Please be prompt!

Formal Attire...Black Tie*

*but no tie...Tom dislikes ties

The invitation to the "black no-tie" birthday anniversary party Herman Chanen threw for me. It really was fancy.

For once, I was fooled. My twin daughters got me to the 1987 birthday party by telling me we all were going to see one of the Disney movies I helped make 40 years ago. I arrived at the Arizona Biltmore wearing an old sheepskin coat. That's Elliott Roosevelt on the left.

There were many close friends there. This is Monsignor Bob Donohoe.

And my life-saver, Dr. Ted Diethrich. That's Attorney Joe Melczer in the center.

Chief entertainer at the party was my long-time friend Wayne Newton. Earlier the same day he had performed for President and Mrs. Reagan at The White House, which he left early to fly in his private jet to get to the our doings in time.

The birthday cake rose pretty high.

My long-time chief assistant Audrey Herring at the party.

And housekeeper Leah Shirk was there, too.

An Evening With Tom Chauncey

Menu

Timbale of Scottish Salmon Mousse and Maine Lobster Medallion
on Dill Verte Sauce, Red Pepper Coulis
Meursault Geneviere P. Morey, 1984

Essence of Saffroned Squab with Gold Leaf
and Herb Cheese Puff Bow

Hickory Smoked Mallard Duck Breast
Irish Lingonberries, Duck Julies
Gevery Chambertin Drouhin, 1981

Three Flavored Fruit Ices
in Dorchester Almond Shell on Lemon Cream

Roast Lamb Rack Bressanne
Sauce Natural with Truffles
Bouquetiere of Vegetables
Potato Basket Parisienne
Chateau Ducru Beaucaillou (St. Julien), 1979

Dandelion Greens with Stuffed Belgian Endive
Persian Pistachio Cheddar Cheese
and Walnut Cherry Wine Vinegar Dressing
Vintage Porto, 1970

Poached Ruby Bartlett Pears
on Savarin Chardonnay Mousse
With Brachetto Wine Fig Sauce

Joyeux Anniversaire a la Chauncey
Taittinger "La Francaise"

Assorted Friandise
Demitasse and Tea

Roses and Cordials

Executive Chef
Siegbert Wendler
1986 Chef of the Year Award
Arizona Chef Association

The Arizona Biltmore   Monday, January 19, 1987

In the office at the ranch, ribbons from horse shows. Thousands of them, maybe tens of thousands. Chauncey Arabians have won titles and championships worldwide.

With a couple of my friends in The White House. That's Bob Goldwater in the middle.

what the hell to do. I was all hands and feet. I felt embarrassed. I got on and sat down and here they are. Beautiful table set.

And this guy who was so critical was dying. I had made him go with me. He had said, they'd never do that in this country. Nobody is going to pay attention to you. Why would the President give you his yacht? He was just stupid. He had me believing it for a while. But sure enough it was there and sure enough we had one hell of an evening. Music. Dinner. Beautiful cruise.

We were on the yacht several hours. As long as I wanted it. I could have been there to the next day.

♦

After I returned from Nigeria I reported to the Secretary of the Treasury. I knew I always had access to President Eisenhower if I wanted. But you don't call people like that. I always knew he was a friend. I had great respect for him and he liked me.

I'd hear from the Governor every once in a while. That was a sad situation because I loved her, Todd. On that trip, that's when their son disappeared someplace on the shores of New Guinea and they lost him, and when they came back they filed for divorce. But you never knew it being with them. They were both a perfect lady and gentleman. They were very dear to us. They were extremely kind to us in every way. Nice people.

♦

John Kennedy was a special kind of guy, of course, and I met him through Senator Hayden. The Senator's golden anniversary was coming up in Congress, and no one else had ever served that long. And Joe Duke, who was from Phoenix and who was sergeant-of-arms in the United States Senate and had been there for many years, was a friend.

Joe called me one day and he said, the Senator is going to have his golden anniversary and do you have any ideas? They'll do something in Washington but maybe we could do something in Phoenix. And he said, do you have any suggestions?

And I said, yeah. The first is we get Jimmy Minotto and see if he'll be chairman.

And he says, no. The Senator wants you to be chairman.

I said, if the Senator wants me to be chairman, I'll be chairman. I can't do it without Jimmy Minotto though, because he's protocol. So we got a hold of Jimmy and said, Jimmy, we're going to do a thing for the Senator and I'd like you to help me. And he said, I'd love to do it.

So we started practically living together every day, putting this thing together. And we started getting names and ideas.

104 The first thing we had to do was to get the President to see if he'd be here. We called him. He said, I'd be delighted for Senator Hayden.

It took about three minutes to get through to the President. Just lucky. Used the Senator's name, of course. And he was delighted. So from there you've got the Secretary of Treasury. You've got the U.S. Supreme Court Justices. Several of them came. Mike Mansfield, who was in the Senate, the others from the Senate, the House. The Vice President, Lyndon Johnson. They were all here. And they were delightful. Twelve hundred people and standing room only and it was probably the first $100-a-plate dinner.

We decided that we wanted everybody represented so we got a flag from each state and that was the worst job of all. They all wanted to get paid. The President's coming here, we want to borrow a flag we told them. We had them around the whole room.

◆

I had called Monsignor Donohoe and said, Monsignor, I'll give you the job of the benediction if you want it. He said, oh boy. I said, one understanding. Ten words or less. I mean it. He said, you've got to be kidding. Nobody says that. I said, Monsignor, if you want the job, ten words or less. Now remember Cardinal Spellman at the Kennedy inauguration praying so long, remember how embarrassing that was and all those people standing there, a lot of them bareheaded in that freezing cold. I'm thinking of you as much as I am us. He said, Tom,

I'll do it, but wait a minute. That's the Bishop's job. I said, I don't want the Bishop, I want you. I could speak that way. I'd known him from Nogales days when I was on a Knights of Columbus team that went down to induct him. He was honorary chaplain or something. That was about fifty years ago.

After the dinner, I introduced the President and he got up and he thanked me and he said, Senator, I remember when I came to the Senate the first time and I walked over to you after my first session and I said, Senator, how does it compare now with when you came here as a young man?

He says, young man, when I came to the Senate, young Senators didn't speak. Now, he said, Senator, that's on the record. Apparently Kennedy got up and spoke when he should have kept his mouth shut. And he told him, a young man didn't speak. The President was just delighted and he went on with some very lovely stories.

That was the first time I had been with the President and he said to me when it was over, I thanked him for coming and so on, and he said, no. I want you to come up to my quarters with me. And I said, well, Mr. President, I know you've had a long day. He said, I want you to come up to my quarters with me. So when we go, you go with me.

We had a problem, we always had problems with staff at the White House. We were outlining what we were going to do and I had said, Jimmy, we ought to do something about the kids. How many kids in journalism school would ever get a chance to meet the President of the United States? Let's have a kids conference with the President. He said, you can't do that. I said, why can't we? If the President agrees to it we can do it.

But we get a call from Kennedy's staff right away, you can't do that. He won't do that. So I get a hold of the phone and I ask for Senator Hayden and I said, Senator, I've got a problem. We promised a bunch of school-kids that the President would have a press conference here at the hotel and it would be great.

He said, that's a great idea.

But, I said, his staff won't let him do it.

He picks up the phone and he says, get me the White House. I want to talk to the President. It was that quick. Honestly.

105

Senator, what can I do for you? He said, Mr. President, Tom Chauncey —

He said, yeah. I know about Tom.

My chairman tells me that he's promised some kids that you'd do a thing and it's been vetoed by the staff.

He said, where does Mr. Chauncey want me? And when? Tell him it will be taken care of and we'll be there. Thank you very much. Thanks for all the work you're doing. I'll be looking forward to seeing you.

Then another problem develops. We've got the motorcade and we have to take the Senator to the Westward Ho on that north side by the post office and let the Senator out and

106 let him go into his hotel and take the President on to someplace else. And here again they said, you can't do that. You can't stop that motorcade and let the Senator out. He'll have to go on with the President until it's over.

Well, get on the phone. The President was right there and he said, we won't stop and let the Senator out. We'll stop and I'll escort him to his quarters. We stopped sure as hell right there. He got out, opened the door, took the Senator by the arm, walked to the elevators, took him up to the room, came back down and joined us. That's the kind of a man he was.

When he and I got to his suite the very first thing the President did, he called his father and talked to him five or ten minutes, told him what had happened during the day.

Kennedy was a handsome man. Looked you right square in the eye and was extremely courteous and proper. He put you at ease immediately. Easy to talk to. Made you feel like you were king, that you were the most important person in the world. We spent most of the Carl Hayden dinner talking about the value of land in Paradise Valley. He had been here after the Navy, the family was here for recuperation and a get together. What he wanted to know was what the land was worth now in certain places. It was the land that became Paradise Valley Country Club. He thought that would have been a good piece of land and he should have bought it. This is what we visited about most of the time. Very interested in Arizona. He believed in it.

He put himself right at your level real quick. I never felt, you know, here's an eighth grade kid sitting with the President at the dinner talking about what's going on in the world.

♦

I had gotten a call from Stewart Udall. I'm not sure whether he was a Congressman or Secretary of the Interior at the time, it was one of the two.

He said, Tom, I need to meet with the President.

And I said, boy, stand in line. The pressure's terrible.

He said, I would consider it a great favor if you could arrange so that I could see him, if I could have five minutes.

I said, I'll see what I can do and I'll try. We'd been friends **107** for years. We respected and liked each other. I got along with the Udalls. Mo and Stewart both. I knew their grandfather, their father, well, they're old friends. So I called the President, I didn't ask the staff. I'd already learned that much, if nothing else, from this thing. I said, Mr. President, when you're here, Stewart Udall would like five minutes. He says, all right. Set the time where we can get it into our schedule.

I knew better than to ask the staff. They wouldn't do it. They'd say, see him in Washington. He said, you set the time. If you want me to do that, I'll do it. Period.

I said, well, that's nice of you and I'll get back to you. I'll have a time when you get here that won't interfere with other things. And I said, Mr. President, Mr. Eugene Pulliam, who is a very dear friend of mine, publisher of the paper —. He said, I know Mr. Pulliam. I said, he said he would like a meeting with you for a few minutes. Again, tell me what time and where and I'll have a private meeting with him also.

There was a young kid running around who was hyper-charged. A school-kid. The same request. I got him into the dinner and introduced him, but I did not get him an interview. And it turned out to be Gary Peter Klar, the activist kid, lawyer. Very bright, precocious. He was a youngster of course then. And I did get him so he could meet the President.

What Udall wanted was, Stewart Udall represented McCullough. McCullough wanted to buy state and federal land at Havasu and build a city. And of course he would build a first-class city and create jobs. So he wanted a lot of land and he had gotten no place. That night he and the President concluded the government would not resist a fair and equitable sale of land if they were indeed going to build a city and create jobs and do something at Havasu City. I've never told this story to anyone. Nobody knows about it, but I did set it up. Kennedy did agree and later, McCulloch bought a lot of acreage and bought the London Bridge and built Lake Havasu.

♦

For that dinner, I had wanted someone to entertain the President. You know, that's a difficult thing to do. Most of all, people are scared to death. But Danny Thomas and I had been friends for quite a long time, and he was a great entertainer so I called him.

I said, I want a favor.

What?

I want you to come and entertain a couple hundred people.

That will cost you money.

No it won't. It will cost *you* money if you don't do it.

How do you figure that?

Well, first of all, I'm chairman of a dinner, we're going to have the President of the United States.

You're kidding. How are you going to do that?

It's already done. He'll be here.

Well, that's kind of hard to do.

And I said, and not only that, the Vice President will be here. A lot of the Supreme Court justices, a lot of the Senate. I said, this will probably be the seat of government for a couple of days.

He said, when is this? I told him. He said, on one condition. No money. I don't have any money to pay you. Nobody gets paid.

One condition. I have a dream and I want to build a hospital for children. And we're going to call it St. Jude's. But I'm not getting anyplace. I need to see the President. I want five minutes with him.

108

You guys and your five minutes. The poor guy is going to have to stay here until Christmas. But I said, I'll try. I promise you I'll try.

So when the President turned to me after the dinner and said, you're going to come upstairs with me, I said, Mr. President, I'd like to bring Danny Thomas with me. He wants to talk to you.

He said, fine. Bring him with you.

That night, he talked to the President, got his support for St. Jude's. Danny Thomas wasn't there five minutes. Probably doesn't even remember me in the case. He really was excited. Stepping all over himself in front of the President. I've never seen him so nonplused in my life. And he did a great job of entertaining. But scared to death when he was face-to-face with the President.   **109**

When we finally were alone, the President and I talked about everything. Just everything. I think conversation with the President of the United States is privileged and private, so the only thing I can tell you is he knew more about me than I knew about him. Somebody had done a real nice field job. He knew all about me. How many kids I had. That I had come out here on a freight train. That I'd been very poor. I'm not so sure but I think he knew that I was a life member of the Hoboes of America, something I'm very proud of. He knew what time I got up. What time I went to bed. He must of gotten that through the Secret Service.

At the dinner, we liked each other immediately. He sat there next to me at the head table that night and re-wrote his speech. Entirely different than what he was going to say.

♦

After the celebration here I heard from President Kennedy quite frequently. I have several hand-written letters, not typed letters, from him. Very nice letters. I had written a book, which I had forgotten about, about television, a short book, and he asked me to send it to him, which I did. One of the letters says, I've read your book, and it was a very lovely letter and a very thoughtful letter.

First he called me Mr. Chauncey and nothing but Mr. Chauncey because he was very proper. Then Dear Tom. But I never called him John, ever.

One letter was talking about land values in Arizona. He wished he had bought land when he was here as a youngster. That's great insight. Some people thought he was a spendy kid. He was no spendy kid, he was quite a man. He was a lovely man. I became very fond of him.

President Kennedy was special. But I never cared for Bobby Kennedy. I didn't know him, so that's probably one of the reasons why. And I thought from what I had read, I didn't know that much so it's unfair, I think I liked his brother so much, the President; I think people were afraid of Bobby. I was afraid of him as President. Then maybe a year ago there was a story on Robert Kennedy, the man, on television. I saw things about him there that I'd never seen before. And I completely changed my mind about him. He was quite a man. I think he was probably abrasive, different than his brother and that affected how I felt. I'm happy to say that I was wrong about him. He would have been a great President.

Like so many people, like Barry Goldwater, who's a great man, people never really knew what they were like. They just heard the negatives all the time.

◆

My first acquaintance with Lyndon Johnson was when he ran for Congress and was elected by a handful of votes. I got to know him way back then because I was a partner with Gene Autry. Sam Rayburn, Speaker of the House, called and said, Lyndon Johnson is losing this election. And if Gene Autry will come appear with him in a couple of places, maybe he can win it. It's going to be a close call. But we need somebody to get the crowds to help him. And Gene went back there and it did help him. He won by a handful of votes. When he was Vice President he called and asked us back, and Gene and I arrived at a time when the Congress was in session and we had no appointment, no nothing, and Vice President Johnson said, please have them sit down, take them in my quarters. Took us all in. Gene and I and somebody else. And he just had the Congress take a recess. Sat in there and talked to us for an hour while all the Congress was waiting. I didn't have much respect for that. I said, Mr. Vice President, we can come back another time.

Oh no, he said, I'm glad to visit with you.

We talked about everything, cattle, horses, how close the election had been. How good a friend Gene was to him. How much he liked him. How terrible broadcasting was, how we ought to improve it, which meant giving him more time. Later, he was the President that called Dr. Stanton on a damn near daily basis and complained about every news story that was on the air. And Dr. Stanton would listen to him and say, I'll remind you that we don't interfere with news. They have certain guidelines they're supposed to do and they're supposed to cover the story fairly, Mr. President. We hire the people, we pay them, we give them guidelines, we don't interfere. We neither instigate a story nor do we kill a story. They are there to do a job. They must be fair. They must abide by the rules, but we will not interfere.

Lyndon Johnson was a great one to, you know, he would always put his arm around you when he talked to you, when he wanted a confidential talk. Pressing the flesh he called it. He was terribly nice to us, but I never trusted him completely. I thought he was self-serving.

In Austin, Texas for years the only television station in town belonged to Lyndon Johnson's wife. Cable, that whole bit. And they had a dear friend of mine manage it named Jesse Kellum when I was on the board of CBS affiliates. Jesse Kellum represented that district, and he was a fine man, he ran a good station. But nobody, nobody, ever got another station in there while Johnson was president. And he was very blatant about it. It was a bad thing. And the talk of the industry. I didn't have much respect for that. It wouldn't have hurt him to have had some competition. It was in Mrs. Johnson's name. That was the subterfuge to begin with.

When President Kennedy died, those bills that President Johnson passed were President Kennedy's. Bills and ideas. He rode on the coattails of President Kennedy. But he was not highly respected amongst the inner circle.

♦

I met President Nixon, went to his house on the west coast once. I was invited and they met me with the helicopter

111

in Los Angeles. There were several people there. I think Princess Margaret was there at that time. And Mason Walsh, maybe. He just invited some people from Arizona to lunch. Easy to know, but very aloof. Unfortunately, when you were in a room with him, he was a loner, I thought. Instead of looking you in the eye when you were shaking hands, he was looking over your shoulder to see who was next. Which is a bad habit.

♦

I liked President Ford. I met him. He was nice to me. I don't know him well. I don't think he'd know me if he saw me again. But I think he was President at a very bad time and I think he handled it very well. I have great respect for him. And his wife certainly faced up to her problems without trying to hide.

I think the highest marks you can give President Ford is that he was a great Congressman. He was. Obviously. He was a good President and he sure took a bad time and I think he healed a lot of problems in this country by the very low-key effort. It was awful the way they made fun of him bumping his head and the stupid things they did. He was President of the United States of America and he carried it very well. He was never cocky. He was humble. They had kids. They treated them like kids. They didn't try to hide their weaknesses, their good sides. I'm sure they loved them dearly. They handled themselves well. It's tough on kids to have their parents in the White House.

♦

I knew President Carter but I never really knew him. Strange. The only time I think that's ever happened to me. Long before he ran for office, we got a call at the station one day that Jimmy Carter wanted to talk to me. Apparently, throughout the months before he ran and before it was announced, President Carter would call people in different communities and want to get acquainted with them. I think it was a plan, and I just happened to be in the broadcast business. I doubt that it had as much to do with me as it did the job I had in broadcasting.

He said he just wanted to say hello. Wanted to come to Phoenix. Would like to visit sometime when he's there. That sort of a goal. It was the only time that I really talked with him.

Then he sold the boat, which made me mad. You know, the Sequoia. A great historical thing and it was President Roosevelt's, and I had been fortunate enough to have it one night for dinner. It costs practically nothing and it helped train new servicemen.

And he sold it and it was a treasure. He was a Navy man himself and I think some do-gooders told him that it probably would be well to get rid of it and not have it. Well, it was a great place to take people to dinner.

What if you get the President of Spain or France? How better to entertain them than to take them, four or five people on that yacht and go up and down the Potomac and look at all of those great monuments? It gives you room to talk about the history of America because it's all right there. The Jeffersons. The Lees. The Washingtons. The Lincolns. A lovely trip with a candlelight dinner and soft music. It was a great place to spend two or three hours. I thought selling it was stupid.

113

♦

I met the Reagans when they were married. Her mother and father, who is her step-father, but he adopted her, Loyal Davis, used to come to the Biltmore, and he loved horses and he rode horseback every day. And they always had an Easter party, forever. I was at their house a lot. On my way home I'd just stop in till the day they both passed away. And we were dear friends. Close personal friends.

When we wanted to build Barrow Neurological Institute, I was one of the incorporators, one of the founders. I called Dr. Loyal Davis who was the head of neurosurgery at Northwestern University. And I said, Doctor, I'd met him at those Easter parties, I said, we're trying to start this. Will you help us? Will you be on the committee? He said, not only will I help you, I'll give you a bunch of my papers. Yes, I'd be glad to help. And he did. And we became very close and I spent quite a bit of time with them and Nancy. That's even before Ron was Governor.

When the Reagans came to town we'd have dinner, we'd have lunch or they'd come to my house. They came to my house when he was Governor to have dinner. And we showed him the horses. He loves the Arabian horses. He'd ride every day, as did Dr. Davis until he was seventy-some years of age. That's the way we became very close.

President Reagan is an excellent horseman. Rides a flat saddle, which I couldn't do very well. You've got nothing to hang on to. A flat saddle, we call them pancake saddles, no horn to hang on to. An English saddle. He'll ride all day. He really is a good horseman.

I've seen the Reagans in the White House. They invited me back for a dinner, Bob Goldwater and myself, the attorney Vincent Zepp, who handled the stuff for Mrs. Reagan's mother, and one other person. Went back for that dinner and they were terribly nice to me. Extremely nice. I have a standing invitation, which is very rare. All I have to do is pick up the phone. I'll be sitting here at times and the phone will ring and he'll say, Tom, this is Ron. And we visit. Also, I've called him in the White House. Takes me about three minutes, usually. I have never waited on a call to either one of them. And I've always said when I put the call in, I have their private numbers, it is not urgent because the time I called them mostly, her Mother was still living and I didn't want to frighten her. And I'd always say, it's not important or it's not urgent. The switchboard people know me and they know I have access. And it's immediate.

I've never asked him to appoint anybody or anything. I've heard him speak, I thought most of it was good. If there was something I didn't think was the best I'd say so. We're friends. Just like I talk to you about the same things, only they're in Washington and I'm here. Loves horses and I think they have two or three of mine I gave them. As soon as he gets out he's got another one coming.

Do you know what she said to me? If that horse hurts him I'll kill you. That's exactly what she said. She said, you be sure he's gentle. I said, you bet I'll be sure he's gentle. She said, well, if he hurts him I'm going to kill you. I said, thanks for the compliment. That's exactly what she said. And I'll guarantee you he'll be gentle.

Nancy Reagan. She's beautiful, good looking. You immediately like the First Lady. She is warm, she is caring.

So I cannot believe what I heard yesterday that she runs him around and tells him what to do. Anybody that's ever

114

known Ronald Reagan or the First Lady, nobody tells either one of them what to do, including each other. They have a great love and a great relationship. No way either one of them can tell anybody, either one of them what to do.

This is my reaction to the Donald Regan book. No way in the world that that lady is going to tell him what to do or what to think. They both are independent thinkers and they love each other dearly. It's a great romance. It's one of the greatest romances I've ever known. And I'll guarantee you, it's a great romance because neither one of them tells the other what to do. They'll discuss a lot of things.

I've never heard her mention the stars in all the years that I've known her. Never mentioned astrology. My stock answer to astrology is that if you believe in God, it's pretty hard to believe that way in the stars. I don't know whether that's right or not but that's just my impression.

I think Mr. Regan is just too sour and I think it's just too bad that a man who's had that great trust in the twilight of his life would destroy his reputation. I think it's too bad that he's so bitter.

I've been around them too long. If they were that dependent on stars I'd have certainly known it. I've never heard them mention it.

◆

One story about Mrs. Davis.

Merv Griffin came to town one day, and he and I are very good friends. He was raising money for the hospice, Gardner's Tennis Ranch, and I said, Merv, your old friend is here and she's not too well, you and I ought to go see her. He said, who's that? I said, Lucky Davis. Oh, he said, I'd love to see her. They all called her Lucky back then. Her name was Edie Davis. So I called and said, Merv's here and she said, I'll see him. I said, we'll be right over.

We went in and she's visiting with Merv and they're glad. They're talking about old times and all, they knew each other in Chicago and this and that. And he was telling her who was there and that's nice, that's nice, she says. She's sitting in a wheelchair and she's not very old and she's still sharp as hell and they're just having a lovely time. And he says, and Senator Charles Percy's there. And she says, who? And he says, Chuck Percy is there. She says, he's a horse's ass. Stuffy. Just a bore. And Griffin I thought would fall down laughing. That's exactly what she said.

◆

I don't call Ronald Reagan Ron anymore even after knowing him thirty or forty years. He is Mr. President. She's the First Lady. I call her Mrs. President, not Nancy. Never. She is Mrs. President to me. Of course, everybody gets a big laugh out of it because they've never heard of that one. But that's what she is. But I never call him anything but Mr. President. That's what we need in this country. Respect of those offices. It isn't who's in them, it's what's happening in them. And if nothing else the Reagans put some dignity back in the White House.

◆

I've always been a great believer in Lincoln. Fascinated with President Lincoln. And I think in spite of all the heat he took, he really tried to free the slaves. And he did, indeed, free those slaves. He is the man that did it and got killed for it.

He was an imperfect man, I'm sure, like all of us, but he did, early on when it was dangerous to do it, he wanted some freedom and he did do it.

My wildest dream would be to sleep in the Lincoln bed or go and spend an hour in that room. I have an invitation from the Reagans to do that. And before they leave office I'm going back there and spend the night. It would be a great honor and a thrill for me. It may seem silly to a lot of people, but from a child I had great admiration for President Lincoln.

◆

I'm a lifelong Democrat but I became Republican so I could vote for Reagan. When he gets out of office I'm going back to being a Democrat again. I was Democrat all my life. The last time he ran I registered just before the vote as a Republican. I don't like what either one of the parties is doing right now. I think it's terrible the way they're tearing each other up. Sad.

Chapter 8

Gene Autry
and More

I made $100,000,000 for Gene Autry, on one piece of property. Gene and I were as close as any two people could be for forty years. And his wife and I, the three of us were like brother and sister.

I made Gene a lot of deals. The biggest was when I bought KMPC for him. He called me, he was off on location and he couldn't do any good and he asked me to go to Hollywood and meet with a man who was having trouble with his station and it was for sale and he'd like to buy it. But he couldn't do that and would I go do it?

I didn't want to go alone. I was pretty young. And I asked John Rockwell, who was the owner of the Adams Hotel to go with me and I took our manager of the radio station, Charlie Garland, and we had a hell of a time. You couldn't get a flight. So John said, call Charlie. So I called Charlie Garland. I said, Charlie, I'd like you to go with us. The earliest flight in the morning, which is five or six o'clock, and John Rockwell and I and you, and I'm going over and look for, off the record, a station Gene would like us to buy for him. And Charlie said, okay.

As we're getting on the plane, John said, did you have any trouble getting the tickets, Charlie? Charlie said, no, I just told them who you were. Of course, John Rockwell of the hotel put the airline people in rooms all the time.

We got there and had this huge suite in the Knickerbocker Hotel in Hollywood, and here was a fellow named Horace Lohnes, who was one of the deans of federal communications law, and a fellow by the name of Bob Reynolds who was working for this station owner who was in some kind of trouble with the Federal Communications Commission. I don't know what the problem was but it threatened to lose him his station. Anyway, it was for sale.

The deal was that this Reynolds wanted control. And I said, Bob, you will not get control with Gene Autry in the picture. I won't recommend it. We discussed it quite a bit and I said, you won't find a fairer man in the world to deal with than Gene Autry. His word's good. He won't squeeze you out. You'll be treated as a full partner. But he will not come in here and buy the station with his name and have you have control. So he finally agreed to it and we bought it right then and there, right on the floor.

118

We had done all our business on the floor. It was covered — the papers, all the engineering, all the design, all the accounts receivable, the payables. It was just strewn out. It was a mess. But it was a great station in Los Angeles and it was a great frequency.

The real clincher of the thing, the real unbelievable thing is we bought it without any cash. I told Mr. Reynolds we don't have the money now. We'll sign it and guarantee the money and we'll pay $100,000 in six months. And we bought the whole damn thing without a nickel down. And in six months I had a hell of a time getting the money, to raise the money, but anyway we did and Gene said, what part do you want of this? I said, nothing, it's your station. I don't want any part of it. It was an absolutely marvelous piece of property. From that came KTLA.

He called me one day and he said, we've got to sell KOOL-TV or KOLD-TV down in Tucson. I'm in trouble. I need the money. I said, Gene, that's the worst mistake in the world that we could make because they were the only two stations in the country that cover 97 percent of one state. We're on the mountain in Tucson, it's 12,000 feet and we're in Phoenix on the mountain and it's grandfathered in. You'd never get a license like that again.

Well, KOLD is not making enough money.

I fought it for a long time and finally he got an offer of $5,000,000 for it. Now when we bought KOPO, the radio station in Tucson, Gene and I always had handshakes, I was to have whatever part of Tucson that I wanted. Very simple. So I never really worried about it until we started to sell it. And he said, no, it's mostly mine. That wasn't like him at all.

(Earlier, he had called me one day in front of others and he said, I want you to know that I appreciate what you've done for me and I am willing you my part of the Tucson stations. And I said, that's nice. He said, you've earned it. You've saved my neck. You've bailed me out when I had trouble with the bank several times and you've done a great job and it's yours.)

Anyway, now he needed the money and he sold it for $5,000,000. But it's worth $50,000,000. Cost us each $22 ½ million. I don't know what it's worth today. Then it was worth $50,000,000. **119** So that knocked out our total coverage. It was the greatest. We served more people with news than any other entity in this state, including newspapers because of geographics and the quality. It was sad. Gene, unfortunately, listens to too many people some- times when he's not well. He wasn't well. And I finally acceded to it, but it was an awful mistake. It was problems from there on.

◆

Absolutely the number one banker to come to Arizona was Walter B. Bimson. No question that he changed the whole state. He came in the depression. Took over the bank. Everybody thought he was an erudite, too stuffy. He wasn't. He was a very down-to-earth man. The first thing he did, the paper ran, "we have money to loan." He started running ads. Right in the heart of the depression. And it wasn't very long before Walter Bimsom made his mark. And he got the other banks moving.

Walter Bimson believed in people. He didn't loan on statements. He built the Valley Bank that way. This hullabaloo now about writing off these loans to Mexico, that means that you had banks in this community that had a conscience. They were trying to help build Mexico. I don't fault those guys. If they did it and didn't do their homework, that's too bad, there should always be equity when they make a loan. They were doing exactly what they were hired to do, loan money. And that's what they better be doing now, and I think now with our new realignment that that's what they're gonna do.

The danger you have when everybody picks on these loan guys is that they get to where they won't make loans. That's terrible. This community has to have money. That's what a banker does with money. I don't begrudge Mexico a nickel. They owe us a lot of money, we've written a lot off. They'll pay it some day, but I'll tell you, for years it was the other way around. They were putting money up here. They probably still have as much money in our banks as we ever loaned them. They're good customers, so it's not one-sided.

◆

Wherever you'd see something worthwhile going on, you can be sure Herman Chanen was part of it. He was very active in his business, but he was also very active in the community.

Herman joined almost every kind of worthwhile thing that he could do. He wanted to help. United Fund, United Way, any number of them. City of Hope. You name it.

He and I were the ones that fortunately, we put up the money, we got involved in trying to help the inner city. We had done a survey when I was president of the Community Council. A block-by-block survey of the inner city and the thing it showed loud and clear, we needed housing, housing, housing. And it needed, of course, other things but it was a very good survey, complete survey. And Herman went down and worked. Did a lot of work. And I think he's probably been one of the best Regents, the most active they've ever had. He's on the board of the Valley Bank and he's been very active in that.

He's just a fine human being who cares a great deal about his community, as did his Father. So did his Mother. Very charitable people. Not only give their time, but they also give their money.

Herman Chanen is just one of God's very best people.

◆

The Goldwaters of course were quality people. Barry and Bob were treated like dogs by the man that ran the place when they were kids. They were terribly abused by a guy named Sam Wilson.

After their father or whoever it was died, the boys both worked in the store and it was downtown on First Street, and Sam Wilson was just brutal to them. Treated them like dirt. I don't know anybody who knows that but me and probably Harry Rosenzweig. Bob Goldwater is Barry's brother. And Bob has made a great contribution to the state. First of all, Bob was probably one of the number one golfers in the country, and Bob Goldwater was probably on the Valley Bank board longer than anybody in history. And bright and able. Barry got most of the press, but Bob is highly regarded and highly respected throughout the country and a nice guy.

Barry is generous, kind, good, loves his country, loves people. And the whole family were way ahead of the times in human relations. I can remember as a kid, walking into Goldwaters and they had black people in responsible positions. Back in those days. And they had a guy named Milton at home and they treated him like part of the family. True, when they'd have parties and stuff, Milton was always there seeing that everything was taken care of, but Milton was somebody. And it was Bob and Barry, and he was Milton. That's the way it was. And Caroline. They loved him.

I didn't recognize Barry Goldwater the presidential candidate. I think he was captured. There was nothing about Barry Goldwater in that presidential thing that I recognized at all. It wasn't Barry. Not the Barry Goldwater I knew, and know. He was very ahead of his time. There isn't a critical bone in his body about race, religion. He lives and lets live. He's completely ecumenical in every way. The Indians, the blacks, the browns. He was a friend to all of them. I think he probably epitomized what Will Rogers said, he never met a man he didn't like. That's Barry Goldwater.

♦

Clarence Budington Kelland, the author, was a friend of mine. He called me one day and he said, I want to do a story on a broadcasting station. I said, okay. He said, I want to have some intrigue. How does it work? A broadcasting station, how would you jimmy it? How would you kick it off the air? I said, God, what are you going to do? He said, I want to write a

121

mystery, a story. Anyway, he came over and we sat and we talked and talked and he wrote the story. Great writer and a lovely man. Very fond of him. If you didn't know him you thought he was sour. He had a sour puss. But he was a lovely man. And a great writer. We're very good friends.

◆

When I was a kid working at Friedman's, across the street was the First National Bank of Arizona. We were on the southwest corner where Patriots Park is and they were on the southeast corner. Bob Gosnell was a teller making sixty dollars a month and obviously a very bright man, bookkeeper-type, brilliant mind, nice guy.

122

The next thing I heard years later, a fellow by the name of Gosnell had opened a place called the Green Gables, which was at Thomas and 24th or thereabouts. It was a lovely place to eat. Of course, in those days my brother and I had lots of motion picture people and we'd take them out there. We were one of his best customers. He ran a great restaurant, probably one of the best in the country, not just here.

Bob Gosnell always had a knack for quality, everything he touched was quality. And he had a great dream once; he wanted a home in the Biltmore, on that property, and he wanted the home to be different. He was great for heraldry. I don't know whether I was responsible but in some way I got him the lot. Mr. Wrigley wouldn't sell lots. He didn't need to or didn't care, but anyway, he got the lot and I think it was only $15,000 or $20,000, probably $1,000,000 today, and he built what looks like a castle with his crest over it.

The old man flipped and wanted to kill him. He stayed, though, and it became one of the best known houses in the Biltmore Estates, and it was one hell of a house, gorgeous. He planned a lot of it himself. A lot of innovative ideas.

His sons grew up and the rest is history of what they've done. They operated, they took places in town, that one place that nobody in the world thought was worth thirty cents an acre. They bought all that land and they built one of the finest resorts in the world. The Pointe. It's first class. Same tradition of their father and Green Gables. It's gorgeous. It's a credit to any state.

◆

This Mecham thing is all politics. It would not even have continued if it weren't politics. No way. It was strictly politics. And they don't know what they want to do, even amongst themselves. The politicians are fighting amongst themselves.

Republicans don't know who wants to be boss. They're having a hell of a time.

This was a boomerang from Burton Barr being beaten. It was an absolute shock to both the Republicans and the Democrats that Barr was beaten. They can all say, oh it was predictable, but it wasn't predictable. If there was ever a lead pipe cinch to be elected Barr was — and that teaches us a very good lesson. There are no cinches in politics. But there was nobody in their wildest dream believing that Burton Barr would not be right there right now.

123

If it hadn't been for Mecham's personal unpopularity, he would still be governor. There were certain votes against him no matter what they heard in the Senate. I don't care what he said, he didn't have a prayer. Politics is just that strong. You're Republicans and you're Democrats and you stand in line. If you don't play the game you don't share the fruits and the benefits.

It all goes back to one very simple thing, he was not a majority candidate. He didn't win by a majority. He was not the people's choice and politics is a game of the people's choice. So he was easy to attack.

Regardless of whether you like Evan Mecham or anybody else, it's still politics. The issue is politics. Who's going to control the votes and who's going to do what for the next year or two? Who are they going to look to?

Who are the vested interests going to look to? We're going through the worst time in Arizona that I can ever remember. They can call it what they want, but this whole thing is very sad. We are very lucky to have Rose Mofford. She will not only make a great governor, she'll be a great healer. She's capable. I knew her as a young lady who came to town playing softball. Her name was Rosie Perica. She was in high school when I first met her. That's how long I've known the governor. She was a ball-playing wizard, one of the best. She was good. And valedictorian of her class. And pretty. Good, really good. She could play with the best of them. She's a great lady and I've always loved her. She'll be a very good governor.

♦

The president of the network, Bob Wood, called. Tom, we need a favor. We're starting a new show this fall by the name of Jackie Gleason. Jackie Gleason will not ride airplanes so we're putting together a whole train of passengers and on it he will have his musicians and the June Taylor Dancers. It's a long trip. The first place we'd like to have him stop and start him off right is with you in Phoenix. Will you entertain him? Will you do something?

My God. What do you do with Jackie Gleason?

He'll be there two days.

I said, okay. We'll do something.

Right about then Gleason was making a movie for Paramount called *Papa's Delicate Condition*. The studio had built for him a room that was a miniature Toots Shor's. Velvet, gorgeous thing. And when they were through with the picture and since they were all friends of mine, I said, I would like to have that Toots Shor's set.

They said, we never do that.

I said, now wait a minute. Go up and see the boss. Jackie Gleason's coming to town and I have to entertain him. When he comes over here and he sees this damn thing in my building, he's going to wonder who the hell did it. It's got a lot of possibilities and you don't need it.

They said, okay, you can have it.

And we brought it to the studio and we had the bar set up and everything and here comes the guy who picked up Gleason at the railroad and it was 110 in the shade. He had the most gorgeous people you've ever seen in your life with him. All the June Taylor Dancers. He had them all, they were all on this huge train. We picked them up in stagecoaches.

I said, you better take your coat off.

Tom Chauncey

He said, no. I never do that in public.

Mr. Gleason, it is hot.

Yeah. I felt that.

So we put him up on the stagecoach and went all over town, wringing wet, down to my office. And we walked into the patio of my office and here he sees Toots Shor's. Hell, he'd have given me the moon.

He said, how the hell did you get it? So he walked in and had a drink or two. Beautiful thing. Red velvet, gold. And then we went into my office and we had a long visit and then we had to go out to this huge enclosed mall, before Metrocenter came, and you've never seen so many people. It blocked the whole town. And he got up and he did one hell of a talk and entertained those people for about an hour. Delightful guy. It was good for broadcasting and it was good for the community.

In the meantime, I'd invited 600 people for lunch at the Westward Ho Fiesta room and I'd gotten Wayne Newton to drive all night from Vegas so he could play for us, and that resulted in his first big breakthrough nationally when Gleason got him on his show.

Everybody else at that luncheon had steaks and stuff but I sent out and got a giant pizza for Jackie because he's famous for pizzas as big as this table, five feet maybe. He was delighted.

When we put him on the train to leave he said, I've never had a sweeter time in my life.

Later, he wanted to live here. Unfortunately, the Chamber of Commerce wouldn't get off their butt. He wanted to build a house here and live here and play golf. And Florida outdid us, so he went to Florida.

◆

Jesse Owens came to me through a friend by the name of Jack Leonard, who was with *Time-Life* magazine in Chicago, and Jesse wanted to live out here and Jack called me and he said, I'm having a cocktail party for Jesse Owens. Will you come? And I said, sure. I'd love to know him. I'd like to see him. I'm a great admirer of his.

I went and there were not very many people there. There was a little tiddle-tiddle about Jesse Owens being at this fancy

125

cocktail party. He was the honoree. But it passed like all things and he handled himself beautifully. He was a bright, articulate, nice guy. And we became close personal friends. He had a sense of right and wrong. Just a great American.

He said to me, we need to build a surgical center, a hospital, south of the river. Do you realize that when the river overflows, those people can't even get to a hospital? Will you be chairman with me and will you help us get it done? I said, sure. So we became very close and we did build.

At the time he passed away, I had a building, a church that was well-suited, and he wanted to do a participation show with the South Phoenix people on the air and the building I had bought was right across the street from the station on Monroe so it was handy, suitable, for a participation game show of some sort. It was just a half a block away and we were looking into that, he and I.

I was very fond of Jesse Owens. Great, good man. Lovely wife. Lovely family. He contributed a great deal to this community without much fanfare. He was fun to have around.

◆

Gene Pulliam, I met him when he first came to Phoenix. Throughout all the years that he lived here he was one of my dearest and best friends.

Gene Pulliam without a doubt gave away more to charity unbeknownst to anybody than any man I've ever known. He was great for education. The scholarships he gave had to be known because of the paper. But for Gene Pulliam, that was a drop in the bucket of his good works. He was constantly helping something and he was very generous.

Gene Pulliam was a brilliant mind and he was strong-headed. He and I had lots of arguments. For instance, when he came to Phoenix, he charged us for the daily logs, the TV program listings in his newspapers.

I said, wait a minute. He and I had some horrible fights and I said, why would you charge, I finally went to him and said, dammit, why would you charge for the most popular thing in your paper? You're paying for Little Orphan Annie and you're paying for Dear Abby and I said, every time you make a survey the first thing that they tell you they want to have in your paper is the television log.

I said, if you guys keep it up, I'll help build Annenburg into the richest man in the world because he's publishing *TV Guide*. And I said, dammit, it's wrong.

We were dear friends but he was stubborn about it. And I was buying it all and I spent a fortune.

I finally got mad and he was sick in bed. I went out and got the biggest television set I could find and took it up to the house.

He was screaming his head off, don't let him in, don't let him in.

They had security and everything and I said, tell the son of a bitch to lay down and I'll be in there in a minute and I took that set in and set it up and he was hollering all the time. Mad.

I said, you think you know so much about television, how do you know so much? You won't look at it. Now you're sick. You can't get out of bed. Watch it.

And he was hollering all the way out, you're taking advantage of my friendship, that kind of grumble. Well, I didn't hear from him for about a month, he was too busy watching television — and using our logs to find out what was on.

Finally, he said, well that's pretty good, some of it.

I said, now, how about the logs?

He said, well, we'll do something about it.

Shortly after that was the last day I ever was charged. Marvelous man. Good friend. He was right up to a point but he didn't see the total picture.

What he really was mad about, and he had good reason to be mad, is that every radio station in town and every broadcaster in town would pick up the *Republic* and pick up the *Gazette* and they'd take their information and write their news stories out of the paper. Well, hell, he's paying all the bills and they're doing the stories. He was 100 percent right and I said, of course you're right. But it's an infant business. Don't cut off your nose to spite your face. What's going to happen is, the audience is going to see these teasers, we can't put it all on in fifteen, twenty minutes of news a night. You're a hell of a paper. You can expand it. We can't expand our news. The public is going to get interested in the story and then they're going to read your paper.

The only place he and I didn't get along is he tried to teach me to play golf and I was terrible, I was left-handed and I finally told him where to put his golf clubs and left. I tried to play with him several times. They were all disasters. He could sink a putt from nine miles and I'm out there, I can't even hit the green.

◆

I've known Elliott Roosevelt about fifty years. I first knew him when he was in Tucson running McGilpin Field, that airport for Mrs. Isabella Greenway whose husband was a Congressman. And Roosevelt left and he went to all kinds of countries. In the interim he'd been mayor of Miami, Florida. Of course, he was a general and he traveled a great deal with his father. And I hadn't heard from him in years and the McGinns called me one day, Paul McGinn, Mary Ellen McGinn, and said, the Roosevelts are coming to town and they'd love to see you. I said, I'd love to see them. So they had a small group of people at their house.

We visited, old times, and the next time they came they stayed with me at the house. He was there several days. My daughter Sharon and I sat with him one night until three in the morning. I was just simply asking questions. Very nice man. And she's a nice gal and they'd all gone to bed but Sharon and I and the general, Elliott Roosevelt. We sat in the living room.

I've always been curious about Yalta. I always thought that President Roosevelt gave it away to the Russians. So I said, tell us about Yalta. He said, it was very simple. He said, you know Father, he always called him Father, Father was pretty sick. Of course he died and it fell to President Truman, and he said, President Truman was a great President but he didn't know anything about what he was getting into and he certainly wasn't any match, nor would anybody else have been, for Stalin. It was like throwing him to the wolves. Had he been in longer and had a better team, that story would have been entirely different.

It wasn't his fault. He certainly wasn't any match. Father was dead. You can't blame Yalta on Truman or anybody else. It's just that had the President been in there a longer time and experienced, things could have been entirely different, and

128

should have been. I had always thought that President Roosevelt had given it away. But he didn't criticize President Truman. Not one bit. He said, it was an awful mistake to put him in there that quick unprepared. There was no way he could be prepared.

A little known fact about Elliott Roosevelt is that he was President Eisenhower's administrative aide. He was an Eisenhower supporter, which I didn't know until later. Nice guy. Very nice guy.

◆

Frank Snell has no fear. Frank Snell came to Phoenix in the 20s. I met him when he first came here and I don't think there's a day gone by that Frank Snell hasn't tried to help somebody. He doesn't talk about it. Help them or give them advice. And the thing that's so great about Frank Snell, he never knew how to be greedy. Wouldn't know how to be greedy. He treats people very fairly and very honestly. And he's smart as hell. He's extremely smart. Great conscience. He's a great humanitarian. Love him dearly. I could say the same thing for Mark Wilmer.

129

◆

A visionary that nobody ever hears about any more was R.C. Stanford. Judge Stanford was a big, huge man. And they called him an oaf. They said, he's stupid. But he finally became a Chief Justice and we decided that we'd run him for Governor. There was a whispering campaign against him. It was a vile one: Don't vote for that imbecile. He's senile, he's old, he's stupid, he's an oaf. He'll break the country. He's buying all that damn land north of the canal and he's going to be broke, he's going to wreck everybody.

Well, what he was buying is now known as Stanford Drive and the Biltmore and Camelback Inn, that's all he bought! All that land, thousands of acres of it. Every nickel he could get his hands on. And they said he was stupid. He was a visionary.

◆

Del Webb. I knew him first in 1928, when he was a carpenter on the Westward Ho. He hadn't changed a bit. He was still the same son of a bitch when he died as he was when he was a carpenter. The man was a loner, he broke half of the guys he dealt with, the subcontractors. He was a tough, hard worker. But he called me one day and he said, will you have lunch with me? I said, Del, I'll have lunch with anybody. He said, I'd like to talk to you. This was in his later years.

So I went up and met him at that place he owned, that Webb Center or whatever he called it, and everybody in the place was shocked when they saw me walk in, and they were terribly nice to me. Incidentally, I found out his employees all jumped on him as much as anybody about his lousy action in trying to take Channel 10.

I went there and he said, I've got a problem. I said, you've always had a problem. Money isn't going to do you any good. The people just plain don't like you. You've finally found that out. And he said, no, they don't. They really don't like me, do they? I said, no they don't. I said, hell, you ought to know that. You've never done anything to be liked for. All you've done is make money. You're not nice to people. You're not friendly. The only guy that you know that you talk to or who cares about you is the barber at the Phoenix Country Club. (They became friends and they used to play golf. His name was Denny.)

I said, nobody has any reason to like you, Del. You broke an awful lot of subcontractors. You turned the last screw. And you're just not a very nice man. He looked at me and said, what can I do? I said, you can become a nice man. You can get out in this community and give some of those millions away that you earned. You can get into the boys clubs and the girls clubs and the United Way and the Community Council. You have good people. Put them in there and let them go to work to do something for this community. You could build some housing for the poor. You could give some parks.

Well, he wasn't listening. He said, what would you think if I hired a public relations guy? I said, it's not going to do you a bit of good if he tells the truth because you're terrible.

You're not human. You're not nice to people. I said, you enjoy putting people down. I just told him. I said, if you want to do something, change your damn ways. Give some of that money to support some of these things and quit playing games.

What he did, he hired a public relations firm and had them putting out stuff about how good he was. So he called me again and I said, you blew it again. You hired somebody to make you look good. You're supposed to do good, not have somebody make you look good. You know, it's amazing he took it from me. He was ashamed. And I pounded on him but I meant every word I said. He did change before he died and he did do a lot of charitable things. He did try.

The man that really built the Del Webb Corporation and never got the credit for it of course was L.C. Jacobson. He was the guy that built the Del Webb Corporation and he was the one with the innovative, leading-edge ideas. Sun City. Everything. Jake, he was the doer.

◆

That brings to mind Mountain Shadows which is another great story of a fellow by the name of Jim Paul, who went out and built Rawhide. He was a lifeguard in Florida when he came out here and became the lifeguard at Riverside Park, which was the only swimming hole in town in those days. Everybody went to Riverside Park and by the river. A place for dancing. A place for music. A family-oriented atmosphere.

Many years later Jim Paul called me one day. He'd had years of problems trying to get zoning to build Mountain Shadows, a resort. And everybody was fighting him but he finally got it and built it. Of course it was a gorgeous place. He called me one day after it opened and I said, congratulations. I think it's wonderful.

He says, no, wait a minute. You don't know the whole story here. He said, we have no bookkeeping.

You have no what?

We have no records since we opened. No bookkeeping. I don't know who owes me, who we owe, anything. I am about to lose this hotel I think.

My God. How could you do that?

I don't know but I'm in trouble. I need to sell it. Do you know anybody?

Yeah, I think I do.

I thought of Jacobson. I called Jakie and I said, Jake, a friend of mine is in trouble, got Mountain Shadows. He says, oh it's a beautiful place. I said, would you buy it? Here's the story.

He said, I'll get back to you in five minutes. In five he calls and he says, yeah, we'll buy it. How do I get a hold of him?

They bought it, bailed him out. Paul went on then with all that money, made a fortune, and built Mountain Shadows Resorts, the homes. That's the story of Mountain Shadows. Of course Webb benefited greatly, but Jacobson was the bright decision maker.

♦

Frank Lloyd Wright, I loved him. He loved me. We were friends, very good friends. Most people found him a little bit tough, or too hard to get along with. I never did. I really liked the man. And he liked me.

In my jewelry store in the Adams hotel I used on the facing, not very much of it but enough to make a statement, rose travertine marble from Italy. And rose travertine marble is a very gorgeous marble. I just wanted something real for the front of the store instead of rock. We're selling precious stones and precious jewelry and fortunately, John Rockwell went along with me. Anyway, John found it someplace and that's what we did.

Mr. Frank Lloyd Wright, on occasion, would come to the store. He tried to be a sour toughy but he wasn't. He was really a sweetheart. And he always had that pink thing wrapped around his neck, the scarf, and then he had the cape and he had it over his shoulders and he had that fancy hat. He was tapping his cane. And I heard a bunch of tapping going on out in front of the store. I said, what the hell's going on out there? Well, it was Mr. Wright.

He said, what do you mean, what the hell's going on out here? He said, where'd you get this marble?

And I told him.

Well, he says, I want you to know it's gorgeous. Beautiful. He says, can you make something for me and listen to me?

Well, I can listen to you and I can make something for you but I don't know what the hell you want.

I'm having trouble with my eyes. (What he had was a little magnifying glass that was quite thick and he wanted a rim around it, in gold, and a little handle he could put on a chain.)

He had the glass and he said, nobody does these things right. But I heard you do. And the marble doesn't hurt you. It looks like you have good taste.

Mr. Wright, I don't know if I can make what you want or not but we'll sure try. You'll want it in fourteen karat gold.

No. I want it in eighteen.

No you don't want it in eighteen, Mr. Wright. I'll tell you why. Your glass is fairly heavy and eighteen karat is too soft.

You sure?

Mr. Wright, you know more about it than I do. You know the only reason they use eighteen karat gold over in Europe, it's easy to handle, it's more malleable, but it isn't strong. But fourteen would be just gorgeous on this piece, and I can and will make it the way you want it.

All right. I'll leave it with you. When are you coming out?

Soon. So he left it and it was there a long time. He says, you know, if I don't like it, I don't take it.

Get lost, I said, I know that. And we visited about Taliesin West and things were tough, they weren't good in those days. So he went back home. I finally got it finished and it was very pretty. Had a nice heavy cap on it you could put it on a chain so you could wear it and it was very good looking with a little fine rim of gold around the edge of it.

So I called him and I said, your glass is ready.

Any good?

Yes, of course it's good. You're going to love it.

I'll see.

Well, he came down and he looked at it and he says, you know, you'll be successful. You listen. You know when a man wants something, whether you like it or not, you're going to make it the way he wants it. I've tried everyplace to get these things made and they make them the way they want them, not the way I want them. I know what I want. You made it the way I wanted it.

133

And of course, from then on, they'd invite me to dinners. They were just lovely people. I liked them. Mrs. Wright was a dear friend of mine and so was Frank Lloyd. I was very fond of him.

I ran into Swaback, the architect, and he said, I have to see you, Tom. I hadn't seen him in a long time. Several years ago at the corner of Tatum, north on Tatum north of Shea, the Taliesin Foundation built some houses in there. Vernon Swaback, and he had been a student of theirs, and I was curious knowing the family and all that. I wanted to go look at them and they were delightful and pretty. And then I ran into Mrs. Wright someplace and we passed the day and I said to her, you know, I went to see the houses just off of Tatum and they're beautiful. And they've done a wonderful job, congratulations. I think you've done a great job. And she smiled and beamed from ear to ear and she never said anything.

In about three days I had to call the architect, Vern Swaback. He said, I want you to know that you've made a day in my life. We built those and Mrs. Wright wanted to kill me. She didn't think they were any damn good. She was fighting with all of us about those houses. Along you come, you run into her there, and you're looking at them and you told her they're beautiful. You sure saved our day. She must think an awful lot of you.

I said, yeah, we're friends. I wouldn't have said it if I didn't mean it. They're lovely homes.

◆

If I was working on a community council, or the Red Cross, or in the bowels of Phoenix for Salvation Army or United Way, you name it — in a small town you are acquainted with a lot of those people and you do work on a lot of those committees — there were three people that I could guarantee would give money. And I could count on it, if somebody came in with a worthwhile cause, particularly for the humanities, down in that area of town.

Gene Pulliam. Most papers will say they'll give you space, but they don't give you money. He not only gave us money, he pitched in and he'd say, I'm going to put up $5,000 and I'm going to get Walter Bimson to put up $5,000 and Frank

Snell, too. And I could depend on those three just as sure as the sun rose. Never once was I turned down by them. I didn't abuse that kind of confidence and I didn't ask them unless I thought it was something really worthwhile.

I can remember when the bank decided they had to have a committee and they were going to put all this money in a fund and then everyone who wanted money had to go through it, it would be more efficient and they could control it better. Hell, I never bothered with a committee. I'd pick up the phone and call Walter Bimson. And Frank Snell's office did the same thing. They were very generous men, all of them.

It was unfair, really, but it got the job done. I was really unfair to hit them as much as I did. As *we* did. I was just part of a group. You met a lot of people. The luncheon clubs met at the Adams and they figured if you lived there, you knew people. And I lived there a lot, off and on. So you knew almost everybody in the state. It was a really simple door-opener. These men were generous beyond all belief, and always were.

135

◆

I've heard that a lot of people felt that just a few of us, Gene Pulliam and Frank Snell and Walter Bimson and I, had a lot of influence. If you wanted something done you came to us, we were supposed to run Phoenix. Well, I think there were a lot more people that nobody ever heard of who did as much as or more than we ever did.

It just seemed that way because we were high profile. I was in broadcasting and running a news department. Mr. Bimson had a great and fast-growing bank. Mr. Pulliam had two newspapers. And Frank Snell was head of the biggest law firm in the state.

I was in it by virtue of the fact that I lived in the Adams Hotel and happened to know everybody as they came through Phoenix. But all these men had a conscience. They didn't know what the word bigot meant. They didn't know what the word racist meant.

We never really had a meeting. We'd run into each other, or I'd pick up a phone. Remember, Gene Pulliam was across the street one way, Frank Snell was across the street the other, Walter Bimson was next door.

The idea for the Phoenix 40 started when the city was having some trouble and one day Gene Pulliam called and said he'd like to talk with me. He got the four of us together and said you know we need a sounding board, we need to look out in this community and see what's going to be needed. There could be some real problems here with racism, with water, or growth, if they're not cared for right. How do we get people to pay enough attention to see what's needed to be done? Not what we think we want to do, but what they want to do. Why don't we think of some names?

Each of us put a bunch of names together, people who had a track record of community service, not necessarily with **136** money. If they had contributed, fine, but we didn't care how much they had contributed. We were looking for doers. We were looking for people who could bring us information. If we had anything in common, it was belief in community service.

Back in 1950, there was an awful situation in Phoenix. The city was a pretty good old boy town then. They didn't have the cleanest government in the world. There's no question that charter government at that time cleaned it up. But the people in charter government lost their way, probably got too big for their britches. They started telling the folks in Phoenix what to do, how to vote.

Phoenix 40 was never intended for anything like that. Its aim was to seek good people, search out information and be helpful. And not try to run this community or this state. It never was intended to be a social event, ever. I think they made a mistake — and I'm not criticizing them because if you don't like what they're doing, you can stay in there and work yourself, which I did not do — I think they made a mistake when they started socializing, which was not the purpose at all. You're better off if you're not that close. The fact that at the beginning we were acquainted but not close, I think helped it.

I went out of it when Gene Pulliam passed away because I thought it was time for new blood, new people, new ideas.

Am I proud of Phoenix 40? Yes, I am. We took a lot of heat.

We were called elitist. No, we weren't elitist, we had nothing to do with being elite. The members were picked because they had something to offer to help improve the community. And Phoenix 40 did open some doors, and it did make some things better.

Chapter 9

Wayne Newton

There was a time when I was trying to help Wayne Newton get more exposure, so I went to Robert Wood, president of the CBS television network and asked for a Wayne Newton audience, but he said, no, I won't give him an audience, but if you tell me when he's appearing I'll take our people and we'll go to Las Vegas.

I said, that's the only way you're going to see him natural. I think he's the greatest stand-up talent ever known. He gets standing ovations; he's crowded every night. They don't do that because they love him. They do it because of his talent. I hope that you will go listen to him.

So he took a number of people on a plane with him to Vegas. I arranged the seats. And he met with Wayne and Wayne put on a show. Bob Wood came back to me and he said, you know, he's a great, great talent. He's charismatic.

He had that high falsetto voice. Wayne has a tremendous vocal range, he could go two or three octaves, I don't know how many, I'm not a musician, but he did.

I love Wayne. Wayne's been like a son to me, has been for years. He was very young when he came to work for me. He's not a strange kid to me, he did everything at KOOL, Channel 10, and now he's a rugged son of a gun, he's a big, strong man. But why don't you get him to tell you his own story?

◆

Wayne Newton: I had bronchial asthma as a child and was very, very ill. The doctors finally informed my parents that if I was going to live a fruitful life, much less any future years, they had better try to get me out of Virginia and to Arizona. So my Mother had a brother that lived in Phoenix and my Mother and Father gave away and sold whatever they had to in terms of furniture and those kinds of things to simply raise enough money to get to Arizona.

My brother and I had been in show business in Virginia. I had a local radio show on WDBJ in Roanoke when I was six years old before going to school. We were singing and playing steel guitar. Then we would do weekends traveling with part of the road show of the Grand Ole Opry.

That first summer in Phoenix, that would have been when I was nine, we auditioned for a local talent contest called The Lou King Ranger Show. We passed, and then when we came back to Phoenix a second time, when I was ten, my brother and I went on as kind of regulars on that show for thirty minutes on Saturday morning on Mr. Chauncey's channel, Channel 10.

I used to see this white-haired man kind of stick his head in and out of the studio every now and then. And one day when we were doing the Lou King show I received a note that the owner and general manager of the station wanted to see me. Well, it scared me to death, as you can imagine, because my first thought was, my God, what had I done? And so I went into his office and that was the first time that I had met him personally.

I was the shortest kid to graduate from the eighth grade, so I was not very tall at all. And Mr. Chauncey kind of leaned over his desk and he looked at me and he said, how are you doing, boy? And I said, fine, sir. And he said, I just wanted to tell you that I enjoy your singing. And I said, thank you very much, and I was about ready to wet my pants because I couldn't imagine what this man would want with me. That was my introduction to Tom Chauncey.

◆

I didn't start to grow until I was about eighteen. I grew tall very late. And when my brother and I were on television, he hit his growth early and so he literally had to take off his boots when we did television each week so he wouldn't be so

138

much taller than I was that the camera would have a problem getting us both in the same frame.

◆

I trained parakeets to sit on the neck of my steel guitar when I played and invariably we would lose one in the studio. So the second call I got from him, Mr. Chauncey called me in his office and he says, son, I'm having a problem.

And I said, yes sir?

And he said, I love your work, but the birds have to go.

I said, I realize that they're flying away and staying up in the rafters.

And he said, well, I really kind of brought you in here **139** to tell you again how much I enjoy your work and to suggest only that if you clip their wings, then they wouldn't fly away.

And that's something I hadn't thought of.

So he kind of smiled, realizing I was scared to death.

And I went back to the studio and continued the show and from that point on I did clip the bird's wings and it worked. They wouldn't show up on the news shows live, you know, flying around.

◆

He always represented such tremendous things to me. He represented the epitome of what I thought anybody should be if they were going to be in this industry. When he gave you his word, you could go to the bank on it. I mean, it wasn't, well, let me take it up with the board of directors next week. And the tremendous respect he had from the people that worked for him.

As years went on, we became closer and closer and he truly became a father figure to me, and I started calling him Dad, which I still do today. If you've got your butt-kicking coming, he'll give it to you in no uncertain terms and no mincing words. But when that's over it's, okay, now let's go have a Coke or let's go have a cup of coffee. It's never so demoralizing. Luckily he never had to do that to me. He would suggest to me more than chew me out.

I was always amazed at his compassion. When it came to kids or any charitable function he was right there. And as scared to death as I was of him, it really had very little to do with anything that he might do to me, but just his stature, what he represented to me.

He has this ability to accept people around him and give them a chance to excel at their own expertise. He is not one of those people that says, it's my way or no way. He is one of those people that says, if you don't have a better way, try my way. But if you do have a better way, I'm open to being convinced about it, and then make the decision as to whether or not I want to go with it.

I never have seen Mr. Chauncey at any time since I've known him, which has been 36 years, I have never seen him with ego problems. There wasn't ever a situation I felt could have been handled better, or where he came down on somebody who didn't deserve it.

140

Our contact was an ongoing thing, but never anything very concentrated. He always made me aware that he was aware of what I was doing, kind of like looking over my shoulder to make sure that nobody did very wrong by me.

And it wasn't him sitting me down saying, look, I'm going to protect you. It was never that. It was just that anytime anything went down that could have gotten into problems, he was always there. If we had a sponsor of the show, he always made sure that I knew the sponsor and that they knew that he was fond of me. So it became something of a real protection.

If any shows that had any money came up that he had anything to do with, he would always make sure that they called us to do it, because he knew that my Dad was working two jobs and trying to put two boys through high school. Any way that he could help, he did. But it never was a gratuitous thing, it never was anything that would make us feel less dignified.

We had grocery store openings, we did furniture store openings. I think my brother and I made $160 a week on television and when we would do the weekend things it would run anywhere from maybe $25 up to $75, for probably 20-30 minutes.

◆

An agent had come through Phoenix and had seen me on television and contacted my parents and asked if we would audition for Las Vegas. Well, of course, I was fifteen and under age and my parents were concerned. So the agent assured them that he would get the proper permits and all that for us to be able to work and that I would not be allowed in the casino. And Mr. Chauncey was concerned about the effect of that environment on me. I remember him saying to me one time, are you sure this is what you want to do? And I said, yes sir. I've worked my whole life, you know, nine years of it, a long time. And I said, I think that's where I always wanted to be. He said, you be careful and you stay out of trouble.

If I had been his own flesh and blood, he couldn't have **141** treated me any more like a son.

◆

I stayed in touch with Mr. Chauncey. I'd call him every now and then and he'd call me and say, well, what are you doing? Are you staying out of trouble? Do you need anything? Is there anything I can do? It was kind of a touch-base kind of thing just to let me know that he still was there.

I went to Las Vegas in 1959, and I would come back and forth to Phoenix periodically to just see old friends, if I had a day off. We did six shows a night, six nights a week up there for five years. Of course, it turned out to be seven nights many times because when I cut my first album or if I had to take a day off for illness or anything else, the owner of the place where we were working made us do seven days a week to make up for the day off that we'd missed. My brother and I started at I think $500 a week and we had to pay the union, in those years they had traveling dues, and out of the $500 we had to pay the union $200. There wasn't a lot left to spread around, but it was on a regular basis which helped. I moved my parents from Phoenix to Las Vegas I think about eight or nine months after we went there. My brother and I lived in a motel for those first nine months.

Dad — Mr. Chauncey — used to call me about once every two weeks. He was just close enough to say, is there anything you need? Are you all right? Nothing bad's happening to you, is it?

So then in 1962 I think, he called me in Las Vegas and he said, son, I've gotten myself in the damnedest fix. And he said, Jackie Gleason, you know him.

I said, well, I know of him. Of course, Saturday night was when he was on TV but that also was the big night for Las Vegas and I was always working myself so I said, I only know of him. He said, well, he's coming through on a train ride, believe it or not, and he's going on the air on CBS. I'm in charge of producing a luncheon for him and I have to get entertainment. He said, would you consider? I really hate to ask you this because I know you'd have to drive down here and you have no time off.

142

I said, tell me what it is you need.

Would you come down and perform at the luncheon? And he added, there's a method to my madness.

Of course I will.

Well, I think it will be good for you, he said, I think it will be good for you.

And so we finished work about two in the morning the night before and drove down. The luncheon started at noon and we were to be on stage at one. We did no more than thirty minutes and Mr. Gleason stood up at the end of that performance and said, my God, don't go on any other television show before you go on mine.

Well, I didn't believe it, for openers. I thought, that's really nice of him to say, because there was absolutely no reason to put Wayne Newton on television. I had no hit record. I didn't even have a recording contract at the time. I had never done national television but I was aware of what ratings meant to these people. So I felt that it was just a nice gesture on his part to say something nice to a bunch of young people.

I remember Mr. Chauncey just beaming and I was thrilled because he was so thrilled. In retrospect, and I've never said this to anybody before, I went there purely and totally for Mr. Chauncey. I had heard of Mr. Gleason, but to me he really didn't mean anything because I'd never seen his television show. I didn't realize what a big star he was. As far as I was concerned, if Mr. Chauncey needed me for anything, I was there. And that's why I went back to Phoenix.

Well, obviously, it turned out to be the break of a lifetime because that's literally what started any acceptance that I might have today nationally — that show. I ended up doing about twelve Gleason shows over two years. From that came the Ed Sullivan show, from that came Bobby Darin seeing me on that show and then recording "Danke Schön." On and on and on and on and on.

I remember Dad walking up to me after the Gleason luncheon and he said, are you excited?

I said, yes sir. I think so.

What do you mean, you think so? (Because of course he was fully aware of who Mr. Gleason was.)

And I said, because I don't know where to go from here. **143**

He said, I suggest you get packed and get your butt back to Las Vegas. You have to be on stage tonight!

That's the kind of relationship we've had.

◆

I had always been interested in horses but I didn't know of Dad's great interest in Arabians. I wasn't aware that he went over to the Wrigley ranch on a regular basis and messed with those horses. I just presumed that cattle were the big thing in his life. And so in my late twenties I had just gotten into Arabian horses and I thought I knew it all. And I had found out through my horse trainer that a very famous stallion was going to go up for auction in Scottsdale. The horse had been imported from Poland. So I went to see Dad because I had found out somehow that he knew the McCormicks. And I said, well, they're going to sell this horse by the name of Naborr.

I'm aware of that. Have you some interest in the horse?

Yes sir, I would like to buy him. I think we ought to go into this together.

You and I as partners? (And he had that little gleam in his eye. He knew that I didn't have an awful lot of money to spend on anything.)

Yes sir. Would you consider that?

Well, what do you have in mind?

Why don't we set a top of $25,000 on the horse? The people I've talked to said he'll bring probably between ten and fifteen. (Now this is just complete naivete on my part. And again, Dad kind of smiled.)

Twenty-five thousand. That's $12,500 each.

Yes sir.

Okay. Do you want to come down and bid?

No sir, if they see me the price will go up.

Then I'll go do it for us.

Great.

Top $25,000, right?

Yes sir.

Not $25,000 each?

No sir.

So he laughed and he said, okay. Where will you be?

I'm going to be doing a show in San Francisco, I'll call you from there.

The auction was like the next week. So I called him from San Francisco and I'm on pins and needles and I get him on the phone and he's really excited.

I said, how'd it go?

He said, I don't know.

What do you mean you don't know?

Are you seated?

I am now.

We got our horse.

Wonderful! I was so thrilled.

Now wait, wait, wait. I had to pay a little more than the $25,000.

How much?

He went for $150,000.

Well, my God. You would have thought that, you know, that's more money than I'd ever heard of. And I said, $150,000? And he heard, I think, the despair in my voice.

He said, now wait. I know that we went into this and we were going to put a top on it. I feel responsible for that. If you want half of the horse, I'll put up the $150,000 and you pay me when you can. Or you can back out of it and I'll honor the commitment. Or you can have ten percent of him. You call the shot any way you want.

And I said, Dad, we went into this together and we'll come out of it together. I don't know where I'm going to get the money, but I'll get it.

So that's how we ended up in the horse business together.

◆

We owned Naborr for three years. Then I came to realize that Mr. Chauncey loved the horse a lot more than I loved him. I appreciated him, but my true love and affection went for his son that I had, Aramis.

I knew that every time Naborr left Mr. Chauncey's ranch to come to mine to breed mares, it broke his heart. It was like, if he could have been down there in the next stall he would have.

145

Then one day Mrs. Chauncey came to me and said, would you consider selling your half of Naborr? And I'd never thought about it but I knew that something was going to have to happen because Mr. Chauncey was becoming more and more involved with Naborr every day. And I said, absolutely, but only to him.

She wanted the other half to give to him for his birthday or for Christmas or for some occasion. And she said, I realize that he's appreciated tremendously since Tom and you bought him and he's worth a lot more today than what you paid, so what are you going to want for your half?

I said, I want exactly what I've got in him.

And she said, you're kidding.

No, because Dad would do that for me, too.

And she handed me a blank check that she had made out to me with no figure on it but that she had already signed. And she said, that's what I was prepared to pay.

I said, then fill it in. So she filled in the $75,000 and that's the kind of relationship we've had.

◆

We were shooting a show called "Lifestyles of the Rich and Famous" and they had heard about my relationship with Tom Chauncey and asked if he would consent to do the show. Well, getting him in front of a camera could have been one of the most difficult things I've ever tried. And it could have been the biggest favor I ever asked for because he would have much preferred anything in the world but being in front of that camera, and yet he was wonderful. We shot part of that particular show out at St. John's Indian Mission. He had never been out there and he sees all these kids climbing all over the limousine because they've never seen a limousine. And he started carrying on conversations with some of them and before I knew it, he had given them new pews for the church. He'd given them new windows for the church, and three or four months later he had a bus waiting to take all those children up to Flagstaff because they had never seen snow. And yet if you ask him about any of that stuff, he will just look at you and walk away.

146

◆

If I had not had Tom Chauncey in my life, things would have been very different. Most of the good things that happened to me and the morals and principles and standards by which I've lived and developed over the years are a direct derivative of Tom Chauncey. He has almost been my guardian angel. He's been there for me in every single phase of my life that's been important. And I didn't even have to call him. It wasn't something where I'd pick up the phone and say, I need help on this. It's just that when things were kind of bleak or things were going bad for me, the phone would ring just at the moment when I didn't think I could take it much longer.

He had his own ways of finding out what I was doing, and when I was down in the dumps or when I needed a kick in the pants.

◆

One day when I was talking to him about somebody having said something I didn't particularly like, he looked at me with that little gleam in his eye and he said, son, don't listen yourself into trouble.

I said, what?

Don't listen yourself into trouble. Let it go in one ear and out the other. You don't need that kind of hassle.

What a lesson.

◆

I come in contact with and consider friends of mine President Reagan and the First Lady. There is not a time that I meet the President and First Lady, whether it be in Washington D.C., whether it be a state dinner, or on the campaign trail, or via telephone, that the first words out of their mouths are not, how's Tom? When did you last see him? Is he okay?

◆

He always taught me that if I see injustice around me and I tolerate it, then I'm contributing to it. I find that if I continue to contribute to this injustice, I'm worse than the people that are doing the injustice. Because I know better.

147

◆

I call him Dad. For all practical purposes, he is my Dad. I look to him that way. There isn't anything I feel that I couldn't tell him. The last thing in the world I would ever want him to be is disappointed in me. So that gives you some kind of idea of the affection I have for him. And there isn't anything that he has ever asked me to do or could ask me to do that I wouldn't do without questioning.

He is so much of what the rest of us would settle for being just a little of.

Chapter 10

South Phoenix

A young man came to town by the name of Emmett McLaughlin, and he became Father Emmett, and throughout the years I spent a lot of time with McLaughlin, in fact he converted me to Catholicism. And he was always going into the bowels of Phoenix to try to see if he could help some people. It's not an easy thing because he was run out of there a lot of times.

One day he said to me, there's a grocery store down there. I can get that building for nothing from Safeway. It's closed. It's the heart of the depression. I think they'll sell it to us for peanuts. It's vandalized. It's about a 7 or 8,000 square foot building on a corner lot. It was a terrible eyesore.

I want to build a place and call it St. Monica's Mission. Divide it down the middle. We'll put a wall up and we'll get us a camera if we can get one, we'll get some films and chairs and we'll have movies for these people who can't afford to go to the movies. On the other side I want to build a church. Small, not fancy, but a start.

There was an old, junky building next to it and he said, I want to make that a free venereal clinic. Do you know these people are all coming up to town and working and a lot of them have syphilis and a lot of them have gonorrhea and he said they're passing this stuff along to others. Nobody is doing anything about it.

So we're going to get some of these doctors. Dr. Preston Brown and Dr. Hank Running, there were dozens of them, all good men. In those days you knew every doctor in town. The

Professional Building, which is the building south of Valley Bank, was all doctors. We'll get them to volunteer. The gal who gives the shots and stuff, we'll hire her. We'll have to go get the people for the shots because they won't show up if we don't. They're afraid. They're not trusting.

After not very long, we had them lined up around the block getting free shots. Medicine was donated. And lots of those doctors gave their time. The clinic was nothing to look at. It was a little bitty old building. But the nurse gal with the shots, she was tough. If they didn't show up, she'd go over to their house and grab them by the ear and pull them in. And we started the first free venereal clinic.

150

We got the building divided all with volunteer help. Got a movie projector, got some films from the movie studios for free because of the work I'd done for them. Everybody had a hand in helping but the real guy was Father Emmett. He did all of it. Great, great Franciscan priest.

It was through very tough times. Actually when he went down there, they didn't want any part of him. They felt threatened by him. Some of the ministers were very hostile to him. They were too afraid he was going to take over, and they weren't too fond of Catholics, either.

Up until charter government, South Phoenix really got only what was left over. I don't think they were treated at all well. And in fairness, a lot of them didn't want too much from Phoenix. They liked what they had down there.

Now some areas down there are very pretty, you get beyond the slum part and it's a very attractive part of Phoenix. That Pointe Tapatio that they're doing down there now has really begun to help it tremendously. There's some pretty country down there that used to be great farmland. When I was a kid there were more orange groves and flowers — there still are some, of course. That inner part between is the part that needs help. But it has to be the people doing it and it has to be their project. There are people down there capable of that. We have no right to do that to anybody. But we sure have an obligation to be helpful to them. And they at least ought to get their fair share of the tax dollar.

Many years ago I talked Herman Chanen into going in down there after a study we'd made. I said, they need housing badly. Why don't you form a company and build houses that they can afford? I talked him into it and he did it. Unfortunately, they had no guards and vandals tore them up faster than they could build them. So Herman finally got discouraged and pulled out of there. Whether those folks resented it or misunderstood it, I don't know. He finally just couldn't keep going.

Today, I think if someone would go down there and build houses, I think the citizens would stop anyone from tearing them up. They wouldn't let them. Because they have pride in their community.

There are some wonderful people in that area. Hardship 151 creates pretty good people. An easy life doesn't make the best people. Survivors are the ones who develop compassion and care about other people. The teachers down in that area have to be damn near saints. They don't have to teach down there, they can go somewhere else. But they care. There's quite a resource of people down there.

That area needs fixing up. It's better than it used to be. It's hard to believe it can be that bad right in your own backyard. But it is, and it's not going to go away unless we do something about it.

◆

Later when I had the TV station, I used to ask a group of inner city people — we never called them black people — they were from the inner city because that's where they mostly lived, to meet every so often in my office and we'd talk about what is or what could be a problem. I would give that information to my news people and tell them to go cover those stories and see what they could do to get the people aware. And I think it helped a lot. But nobody outside ever knew it.

The first meeting was pretty hostile. I think maybe the names were given to me by some of our people in the news department we had going down there. We were doing stories down there all the time from the inner city, to the point that some people would say, why do you do that, what are you trying to stir up? We weren't stirring up. We were just showing people what it looked like down there. People needed to know it. We didn't shove it down their throat. We did documentaries about living conditions in South Phoenix.

We had people from that South Phoenix side who fought us over it. They said, you're going to stir up trouble down here. But we did it anyway.

At one time, they were going to run Fr. McLaughlin out of town because they didn't want the Catholics coming down there and taking over their business. The preachers, the ministers, some of the blacks. They didn't want people interfering in their business. They were very suspicious of everybody. Of course, they had good reason. They were very badly ignored in that part of town.

152

We had very dedicated, nice kids who went in there to do the news. I cautioned them, don't get nasty. You go in there with the thought that you're going to try to be helpful.

We were trying to get the city to be more conscious that they needed streets down there just as bad as they needed them on North Central Avenue. They needed plumbing and sanitation. There were unsanitary conditions down there. It was absolutely a slum. From Jefferson and the track south almost to the South mountains, from 19th Avenue to 16th Street, 20th Street. It was a huge area. All along the railroad tracks, all along the river, that was terrible.

◆

We came close to a riot one time in Phoenix, a long time ago. But it never happened.

It was on East Washington, maybe around 24th Street. Milt Graham, then the mayor, went down amongst the people and talked to them. He had been active with us in things we were trying to do to help the inner city. And they knew it. It was stopped because a fellow named Dr. Crump and fellows by the name of Burleigh Rideau, Gus Shaw, George Brooks, all black people, educators who had been active in the community, they really kept it from happening with the assistance of Milt Graham and a few others. There would have been a real riot if it hadn't been for their strength.

A lot of people thought George Brooks was a militant. He wasn't a militant, he just wanted something that was right for people, a decent chance and an opportunity. And when you go down and see what he's built, you understand what he was after. He's feeding elderly people. He's feeding younger people. He's educating. He's doing a lot of good things down there.

There were some great people there who didn't really care about themselves as much as they cared about the community and humanity. I was fortunate enough to know all of them.

The riot almost happened because there were a lot of people who didn't feel that they had rights, that they were treated properly. They felt that they didn't have opportunity. The kids didn't have equal rights. Right in the middle of Washington Street, there was a crowd. Hostile. Hundreds of them. It was tough. It could have been a real fuse. It was a close call. Thank God for George Brooks and those others.

Chapter 11

Horses, Cattle and the Ranches

Horses are the love of my life. Particularly great Arabian horses. I can very humbly say without any reservation that on this ranch at any given time, you will find more world-class Arabian horses than at any other place in the world.

That sounds like bragging but it isn't. It's just simply the fact that at the right place and the right time I was fortunate to have enough money to buy a lot of Bask's daughters, who of course is the world's Number One, and he had a lot of world's Number One mares and that statement is made even though I realize that the Soviet Union, Poland, Australia, the Asian countries, Gulf countries, have all raised horses since prior to Christ. Thousands of years. The Bedouins.

We have more horses of that quality individually owned than anyone else in the world. We still have probably 175 or 180 horses of my own. Around the world most horses of this caliber are owned by governments, countries, syndicates. These are all mine. We have just recently started taking in outside horses for training and of course we've always taken them in for breeding, but that's because of the quality of the studs.

Ben Bask, I don't think there's a better stud in the world today. And that's quite a statement to make but it's a fact. We have him and own him outright. No partnerships. No nothing. Euros, same thing. For Ben Bask, we started out charging $10,000 but with the market being off as it is now we're charging $5,000.

Euros is irreplaceable. Euros was on the track for three-and-a-half years in Warsaw and had an extremely exciting record racing. Owned, of course, by the Polish government. I tried forever to get the horse and could not buy him. They just kept saying, he's not for sale. He's not for sale. He's not for sale. I had a friend over there several times who tried to buy him for me and they kept saying, he's not for sale, not for sale. I pestered them so much and they like me, the Polish people, and the government, because they know I had Naborr here which gave him fame and he was famous, he didn't need me, but I just happened to be the guy that bought him. He was a great horse and he left a great mark, as did Bask. Those two horses will be in the history books forever. And they have a lot of babies to prove it.

Anyway, I pestered them so much that they finally conceded that I could buy the horse for an awful lot of money, all cash, and that I would sign a paper that said he was not guaranteed to be fertile, that he would not breed. And if he would not breed I would not get my money back. I had no recourse. That's the only way they'd sell him.

Of course Dr. Khris and I had some real battles over it. She said, don't do it. Don't do it, it's too risky, especially the Poles with all their hundreds of years of experience, you just don't buy horses like that. If he doesn't breed, if he doesn't produce mares, he's just a gelding, that's all, and geldings are worth only $5,000 or maybe as much as $25,000 even as pretty as he is. Well, I don't know why, I just had to have the horse. I wanted him. I loved him. I thought he was great. And I did buy him.

Then came the horrible job of getting him home. It was winter there and I wanted him out of that country as quickly as possible. The Polish government was absolutely Soviet dominated, but the Soviets knew of me and liked me because of Naborr that came earlier from the Poles but he was bred by the Soviet Union. And also Naborr was the appeasement horse from Russia to Poland when they were trying to get along. It was in the depths of winter that I bought Euros. To get to the place to ship the horse, my men had to go out of Poland through East Germany, and it was the coldest winter in years, forty below, fifty below. And they were stopped twice at the border.

The groom finally took his sweaters and shirts off and put them over the horse's head and he'd go back and he'd rub the ears of the horse, rubbed his ears and rubbed his ears, and the reason was because their ears would break off if they got brittle, they'd freeze and would absolutely break off. And the horse was wonderful, and they just put everything that they had on it themselves, the people.

They finally got across into a free country. They put him in a box like a stable, picked him up with a loader and put him in a 747. And I went out and saw him land in Los Angeles and took him off the plane.

That was a great day. He was gorgeous. He was in excellent health. Right off the track. And beautiful. Went through bitter cold weather. We could have lost him in that storm.

157

How much did I pay for Euros? Can't tell you. I promised. The Polish government doesn't want it published. Why I don't know. It was a lot of money. All cash, too. And it was a sterile horse in their mind. At that time he was sterile. It was an awful risk for that kind of money. But Dr. Khris brought him back and he is a great stud.

◆

Mrs. Fowler McCormick had bought Naborr and brought him to America. She had him several years. She let very few people see him or breed to him. She liked me and I was able to see him a lot and I was crazy about him. So when she died she left it in her will that this horse must be sold at public auction. That was it. No ifs, ands, or buts.

Well, I went to the auction. Wayne Newton and I have been friends for many years. And Wayne said, I have to go to San Francisco, I can't be there. But let's be partners and let's buy the horse.

So I went to the auction and I didn't sit down ringside because everybody would know me. I sat way up in the bleachers in the back corner, and there were syndicates from every place. The world around.

I don't remember where the price started, but I'll tell you one thing, I didn't care where it ended, I was going to own Naborr.

When the horse got to $100,000 something, nobody still knew I was the bidder. I'd nod my head and they'd get the bid. My wife was sitting next to me and didn't know I was the bidder, just didn't know it. The bid against me was the people who had just bought and installed London Bridge at Lake Havasu, Bob McCulloch and his man who was very knowledgeable about horses, a very nice guy.

I think I went from $135,000 or $140,000 and I bid $150,000. And of course there was lots of excitement. It was electrifying. They stopped bidding, fortunately. And when they announced Tom Chauncey, my wife damn near fell off of the fence, she had no idea.

So I went down and claimed the horse and went over to the insurance people. You had to sign up and pay for the horse. And the insurance person said, we never heard of your being a bidder. We got all these names of these syndicates and countries and people, but you never showed anywhere. How come?

I said, well, you don't have to register to bid. I didn't want to.

Then I went to pay for it and the guy said, we never heard of you in this bidding. What happened?

Nothing happened. I bought the horse. I signed for it and excused myself and I went over, I called Clarke Beane, who was the chief executive officer and president of Arizona Bank. Now remember, I'm on the board of Valley Bank, but earlier had been on the board of the Arizona Bank and I had a line of credit with them, and I said, Clarke I need some money.

Okay. How much?

$150,000.

All right. How do you want to pay it back?

Six months, three months. Anything. Whatever's all right.

Okay.

And he was writing you could tell and he said, what's it for?

A horse.

What?

For a horse.

A horse? $150,000?

Yeah. He's nineteen years old.

And there was dead silence. Just absolutely dead silence. I think he said something like, are you all right and I said, I'm perfectly fine. It's a horse called Naborr and I want the horse and I want the money.

He said, all right. If you know what you're doing.

So I went over and signed the papers and these people kept saying, we don't know where the hell you came from. We've got all these people in here signed up to buy this horse and you never surfaced. We didn't know you were an interested buyer, is what they were trying to tell me. And I didn't want them to know it either, because the price would go up. I just figured that it was my business and nobody else's and stupidly, I thought I could buy it without having any press. Well, that notion was ridiculous. The word went around the world.

♦

I can't imagine life without animals. Horses, dogs, cats, cows. It irritates me when people call horses dumb animals. They're not dumb animals. You have one problem. People have to be smarter than the horse. A lot of them just aren't. A horse will outsmart you every time.

Particularly Arabs. The Arab horse has a much bigger brain. They have a wider head. That's where that classical profile comes from. And they have one vertebra less so they have more stamina. If you'll watch 100-mile, 200-mile endurance rides, nine out of ten horses winning will be Arabs.

The Arabian horse infused years ago into the thoroughbred. It's what gave them what they call routers. Up until that time, most of the horses, thoroughbreds, were short runners, sprinters. But they infused Arabians into that blood and that gave them the stamina to go further.

In Europe today, in Poland, all they race is Arabians. Those horses will run much greater distances. A mile and a half, two, three miles. A quarter horse will beat them the first quarter or half a mile. Thoroughbreds will beat them in the first three quarters of a mile. And then the Arabian will take them from there. They're endurance horses.

What happened in this country, unfortunately as some of us breeders have learned, Arabians got a bad name because they were more like ponies. They were tiny. But that was inbreeding. We did the same thing with cattle. In-bred, in-bred until we got dwarfism.

There was a fellow named Bob Aste who is a friend of mine, came to town. Years ago he went to Poland and brought back some new blood and started getting size. And we've been infusing those kinds of horses. They're much prettier. They're gorgeous. Everybody said the Polish horse was not pretty. Well, that's not true. They can be awfully pretty. There's some plain-headed ones, but Euros has a beautiful head. And Bask has a beautiful head. I'll show you baby after baby out there that have classic heads.

The Poles learned from the war with the Turks, the first they'd seen the Arabian horse, and of course those horses were brave and highly spirited and just clobbered them. After the war and in time they went into the deserts of North Africa and started importing Arabian horses. And then the Russians, the Soviet Union, got some of their horses and bred them with the Polish horses. In those countries, horses were usually owned by the government or royalty.

These are the horses that General Patton saved most of when Russia was trying to steal them.

◆

How I had to stop riding is a crazy story. That happened because I hurt my back when I fell 300 feet off a mountain.

There's this thing called the Rancheros Vistadores in Santa Barbara, it's a very lovely ride the first week in May and it's been going on for forty or fifty years. I was invited by a fellow named Newt Bass. O.D. McDaniel, myself, Roy Wayland, there was a bunch of people from Phoenix as well, and it's a very lovely ride of about 400 men.

And I foolishly took a horse that I love very much called Laughing Boy that the Waggoner Ranch from Texas gave me, but he was too young. He was a green horse, he was two years old. And I shouldn't have taken him because he was stud and high bred, and I just didn't ride him enough.

We got over there and there's a trail going from Santa Barbara over the hill into Santa Ynez Valley and it's a narrow ledge, very narrow. Just room for a horse. And there was some man behind me that kept bumping into the rear of my horse. Bumping him. Bumping him. Bumping him.

And I kept saying, please back off. Please back off.

So the next time he bumped he knocked my horse off of the ledge and down we went. When I came to, we weren't all the way down the mountain, we were about half-way, 300 feet. We were standing on a ledge and the horse, I was under him, his legs were quivering. He could have killed me if he'd of moved a foot, and my right ear was gone, it was there on the ground right beside me.

161

Fortunately, two or three people behind or in front of me, I don't know which, there was a famed plastic surgeon by the name of Dr. Norris, Beverly Hills. And he said, don't move him. Get the horse away and they got the horse away and this doctor had some string or something. He had no medication, and he put the ear back on right there, on the trail, in about three hours, four hours. And wrapped me with a towel and we went on into camp.

Of course, they wanted me to go on into the hospital and then I said, no. I said, I came here, this is the first day of the ride, I'm not going to go home.

Now you can't even see where I lost that ear, but you look at the back of it, you can see a lot of patchwork.

I fell 300 feet down the mountainside and have absolutely no memory of it. I remember going off the edge and that's it.

I've been thrown by a horse more times than I can remember. When you get thrown, of course, it's always your fault, not the horse's. First of all you usually get on a horse that shouldn't be gotten on to. He's not ready. That's your first mistake. Then you do foolish things. Spook them. Usually you shouldn't get on a horse until he's ready. The only time I was hurt, well I hurt my back, I still live with that. I got dumped pretty hard one time. But I'd get on anything I could get on. It was usually bareback.

◆

I never worry about Dr. Khris. She's here more than I think she has to be. She built a house on purpose just five minutes from here. She has a very understanding husband and he knows that she's going to be where those horses are if they're sick. I've seen her here four days in a row, never go to bed. She's amazing. She's only thirty-one. She runs the ranch. She's a fine surgeon. She does the shows. Have you ever seen her do the shows? Come out Sunday afternoon at two, except in the summer. You'll be surprised.

She's a teacher. She's a good teacher. And she teaches without making it stuffy. You'll be impressed and you'll see forty of the class horses of the world. No question about it. Two Sunday afternoon. It's after church. It's after brunches. And we'll have from 400-600 people here. That's unheard of. It's free. We invite kids. If we pushed it we could have 1,000 - 2,000. One rainy weekend they had it inside. We still had 400 people. Didn't have a seat left in the place. Seats were all full. They were sitting all along the benches.

How did I find her? I've always tried to hire students. I believe in apprenticeship for education. Then I lived at Equestrian Manor, and we had a vet and we had this girl from Columbia, Missouri, the University of Missouri veterinary school. I was out here every morning about five, I'd be out again in the evenings. I always saw this one girl when I was out here. She was out working with the horses, or doing something with them, every time I came here. I thought, my God, she's here awful long hours. So I asked and they said, oh she's always out. So I met her and I said, I want you to come to work. When do you graduate?

She said, another year.

You have a job if you want it.

Thank you. That's very nice.

Later she told me when we were friends, she said, I thought the old goat was just being nice to me.

Come to find out, Spencer Farms who own Seattle Slew and all those great horses were after her too. Word was around.

U.S. Nationals came along and I called at night. Caught her in the lab at school.

I said, what are you doing?

162

She said, sir, I'm just working.

I meant it about the job and are you going to the Nationals?

Oh, no, sir. I can't go to the Nationals. Too busy.

You mean you don't have a ticket?

Yes. Yes sir.

Well, I'm sending you a ticket and my family will get you a hotel room at the Four Seasons where we're staying and we'll mail the ticket to you tomorrow. Then I never saw her until one day in the lobby at the Four Seasons, I ran into her. Obviously, she was out with all those horses all afternoon.

I said, I want you to come to work.

And she said, I'd like to but I have kind of a commitment.   **163**
Well, I know that you'd like it out there. And I want you to think about it.

Sure enough, when she got through, she did go talk to Spendthrift and she had done the same kind of a job there as she did with me here.

She called me and said, I'd like to come out and see you.

I said, you'll just come out here and go to work. That's what you're going to do. I'm not going to fool around with you anymore. And she did come out and she did go to work. She's been here ever since.

This has been her one job after graduation. Interesting story about her and her mother. Her mother drove a school bus to put her through school. Both of them worked for August Busch of Anheiser-Busch running a place called Grant's Park in the summer. Worked with animals again, veterinarian work, so she's had a world of experience. But this is the first job out of school. She's never had another one. She's the manager here. She's the surgeon, the doctor, she does the previews, she does the shows, she announces them. She does all of it. And she's bright. Married to a delightful guy named Jim West, who was the press guy for Governor Babbitt, and he has a consulting firm downtown.

I never call her to come here. She's here. She's here more than I want her to be. I think she works too hard, frankly. I try to run her off.

If you have a sick horse, or if you have a baby coming, you can't get rid of her. We had two babies last night and she was here, and she was sick as hell, but she was here. She's amazing. She's great. She's dedicated to the horses. She's dedicated to the ranch. My daughters are crazy about her. She's like another one of my kids. A fabulous human being.

◆

I had Naborr nine years. He worked as a stud. And I got more than the $150,000 back. Right away. In fact, if I had known what I know today, we could have done better with him. Had I known more about genetics and mares and the proper mares to breed him with. It was more important for Naborr to breed horses than it was to have heavy stud fees. I priced him too high and I shouldn't have. But you learn that as you go along.

I have seen bus loads of people come from California. They'd call and they'd say, can we come see Naborr? And I'd bring him out and they'd stand around the outside and I'd say, come in. And they still couldn't believe it.

I'd say, go in and pet him. I'd just let him stand there and they'd be all over him and this horse would just stand there and look at them. The tears would roll down from their eyes because you knew you were in something very special in his presence. Some royalty. And he was royal. He never moved. He never raised his foot. His ears were up. He was just standing there very friendly. He was regal. They came from all over the world to see him. He was a special horse. I just wish I'd have known more about breeding at the time, but he left us great legacies. He's got a lot of champions.

We charged $10,000 or maybe even $25,000 but it was way too much. He bred a lot of horses, but he could have bred a lot more at a more reasonable fee. It was ridiculous not to do it. I just didn't know what I was doing. I had a great horse but I didn't know, I wasn't that smart.

◆

Naborr knew me. I could hit this driveway, he'd start chortling when I hit the driveway, so help me. And he was always standing there chortling to me. That was the first place I went when I got out of the car when I got home was go say

164

hello to him. And he knew me from out in the road. He knew the car.

You knew you were in the presence of a very special thing when you were with him. He wasn't a thing. He was a living, breathing doll. A child could go in his stall and crawl under his belly. He wouldn't hurt anybody. He was really a docile, lovely animal. And he was gorgeous. He was a good friend. I had him until he was twenty-eight.

I think he would have lived to thirty-five but some people got careless. He didn't take much care. You know, he was a horse that was never sick. He was very easy to raise. Never sick. He was the light of my life. It wouldn't have surprised me to see him live to thirty-five or forty. Arabians live longer than most horses.   **165**

There's two things about a horse you have to be very careful with. You have to watch the hay that it's not spoiled, that it doesn't have mold. And you have to be sure they're fed at the same time every day. If they have to wait too long, they get frustrated. If they get frustrated then they colic, which is nothing in the world but compaction. I swore that I would never be without a doctor again if I was in the horse business because before Khris, it was like pulling teeth to get a doctor to come out here. You could get them but not soon enough. And the quicker that you can get to a horse or anybody, the quicker they're going to get better. That's true of everything, I guess.

He died too soon. But we all do.

◆

Ben Bask is another story. I bought Ben Bask to help some people out. He was a baby on a mother and there was a forced sale of some sort, problems, and I went and I bought a bunch of horses and amongst them was this little baby. And he didn't look like too much. He was out in a pasture. Anyway, I bought a bunch of horses and raised him and he's a magnificent horse and he and Euros are probably two of the best studs in the world today. I really believe they are and many other people agree with me. There are other great studs, obviously, but usually they're owned by companies, countries, syndicates.

I bought him at an auction in Arizona. He's been far more than I ever dreamed, but he was secondary to the whole package of horses. I bought a lot of horses in a package. It was bad for the industry to have a forced horse sale and I have since learned that one person cannot hold up an industry. It's stupid. But he was the result of trying to be nice to somebody. Anyone could have had him for peanuts. He was cheap.

He's rare. You find horses like that in the Soviet Union; you'll find more of them in Poland than any place else, they are the top breeders. The Egyptians in Egypt. And of course other foreign countries. But there are very few countries with horses of this quality.

The difference between just a horse and a quality horse is a great deal. A couple of hundred thousand dollars, generally. And more important, the conformation, the beauty, the athletic ability. Size. Color.

166

Colors are very important. In the old days the Arabian horse wanted to be white. And he wanted to be white only because of the heat. If you'll put two cars out in front of your house this summer, a white one and a black one or a white one and a maroon, any dark color, and go out in an hour and put your hand on one or the other, you can hold your hand on the white one. It's absolutely cool. The dark one will burn your hand.

The same principle is true of the horses. White clothing is worn in the deserts to reflect the heat. Black and dark colors absorb the heat. You can tell it very graphically on a car.

Right now it's desirable to raise black horses. There are very few of them, very few genes that will produce blacks. In those days past you could hardly sell them. In fact, they disposed of them because they were too hot in battle, they were too hot in the heat of the desert.

You have to remember also that those horses lived in the tent with the Bedouins, just as our dogs live with us. That's one of the reasons Arabians are so people-oriented, family-oriented. Loving. They were part of the family. The reason they lived in the tents is simple, the people didn't want them to get away or stolen, and that was their lifeline to water, wherever they were going, or battle.

The mares were the most prized, always. Not the stallions. You'd think the stallions, but no, always the mares. Of course they're very sensitive. But the mares themselves were, and still are, one of the prized. You can get more from a stallion in syndication because he can breed more mares. If a mare has eight or ten babies, that's a lot. That's really all she should have, assuming that she doesn't get sick or have what we call dirty, pick up stuff out of the air or something that would make her unbreedable.

Horses get sick like people and they become not breedable. They become infertile. They get infected. But you're very careful on a breeding farm. Our farm is as clean as a hospital. That's because of Dr. Khris. She's a fussbudget about absolute sanitary conditions and she's right. We've been very successful raising these horses. On any given day you can come out here and see any of the world's finest horses you'll ever see. They're here. And all under one ownership.

◆

I bought Gardenia for $1,500,000, she was a Naborr daughter. She's absolutely gorgeous. I was thrilled, of course, to have her and a friend of mine from the east came to me several times wanting to buy the horse. I said, no, I won't sell her. The next sale the following February, a year later, he came up to me, his name was Paul Wood, Colonial Farms in Texas, and said, Tom, there's a man here been trying to find a top horse and he wants a world top horse. And he said, we're going to lose him to this industry unless he can buy a great horse like Gardenia. Will you sell her?

I said, no. I don't want to sell her, not for any price. She really is not for sale.

Well, then put a price on her that you think is ridiculous. The man wants to buy a horse and he wants the best and she is the best, there's no question about it.

Oh, $3,000,000.

I'll be back.

The man came and bought the horse. I was just sick. I finally knew what pleasure and pain and sweet and sour meant. Anyway, I delivered the horse and the man fell on hard times and he loved the horse so much. He was a nice man but he'd paid only a million and he owed me a couple million dollars. He had a lot of horses and a lot of debts.

So we started looking for the horse and we had heard the buyer was going bankrupt but he wouldn't return the horse. The horse had a baby, also. We kept calling every place trying to find out where that horse might be. Somewhere in the conversation, Dr. Khris had heard this man say that his father was raising horses in Missouri. And her mother was still in Missouri. She said, you know boss, I think that horse is probably in Missouri. His father's down there, maybe if we could find out where he is, we could get her.

So I took a lawyer, my son, and a sheriff and sent them there, and Dr. Khris, and they found where the father lived. It was out in the boondocks and it was a very scary situation. Fortunately, the father was in town and they walked in and everybody was looking at them. Of course they couldn't find the mare, but way off in the distance they saw a head sticking up and there was no question of who she was. And they had the papers from the judge and they had a gun because they were afraid of trouble. And they walked in and grabbed the mare. They told the lady, showed her the papers, and they put the horse on a trailer and drove off. They never found the baby. We don't know to this day where the baby is.

That's the only reason we got that horse back. We don't think she'd have probably lived long because she was in a different atmosphere, after she was so pampered here.

Our people got her in a trailer and headed for the next town, then telephoned me. They said, we got the horse. But when the old man gets back, that will be dangerous. We're afraid. They take their horses serious down in this country. We don't know what to expect.

I said, you just take the horse, keep it out of sight, and drive as fast as you can to get across that state border and that's what they did. I sure sighed with relief when the horse pulled in here.

A friend of mine, Paul Paliaffito, a very nice guy in Wisconsin, bought her from me. But we have no idea where her baby is. We'll find it some day because they can't do anything with it, it's not registerable. She's probably almost three years old now.

◆

One horse given me by Guy Waggoner was huge. He was the horse that James Arness and John Wayne used to ride. He was that big buckskin and had that black thing down the ridge. He was tall, he was sixteen hands. He had to be tall for those big guys. They're both over 6'4", 6'5", they needed a big horse. And I loaned the horse to Gene. They made Gunsmoke out at Autry's, he owned that place in Newhall that had the western street deal, the old western town.

They had to have a horse big enough for Arness and for the Gunsmoke series which they made a lot of. And I loaned him a horse named King, which the Waggoners had given me. That horse was probably in more pictures than John Wayne and Arness put together. He was a great horse. He came back and he died on my ranch up at Winslow. He was retired up there.

169

♦

I had one fight with Mrs. McCormick in all the years I knew her. When she owned Naborr, we had a mare that I bought from the Wrigley family for pretty good money, in fact they charged me $1,000 more than they had it on the sale for just because I wanted the horse. I never got over that, either. Anyway, she was a great mare and I called Mrs. McCormick and I said, I'd sure like to breed Warda to Naborr.

Fine. $1,000.

Oh, that's fine.

You bring her over and we'll breed her for you.

That's fine, Mrs. McCormick. Thank you very much.

So I took her, they bred her, of course it didn't take. She sent her home.

And I called her, I said, Mrs. McCormick, can I bring her back?

No. Once is all you get.

Mrs. McCormick, you never get a horse on the first time, it's rare.

That's all. You owe me $1,000.

I didn't even get the horse bred. You don't get any money.

Yes I do, and she hung up on me, madder than hell.

I got a wire from her: To Mr. Tom Chauncey. You're just like my son, you're no damn good. Send the $1,000. Signed Ann McCormick.

She was in the famous McCormick family, McCormick Deering, McCormick International Harvester. Immense wealth. Still she wanted that $1,000. I never paid.

♦

Every horse is different, like children. It depends on attitude. Generally, the Arabian horse is very teachable because they're very smart. They're intelligent and they respond to kindness. We do not get on a horse's back until they're three years old, because Arabians develop slower and they live longer. We hand drive them, hand walk them, and handle them a lot. And after three on, I would say, to make a horse it'll take about a year from the time you start. Some will come quicker, some will be slower. It's a long process. And it's every day.

You can tell a horse is smart by their reaction to what you do with them. Most Arabians are very intelligent. They have a wider head set, wider between the eyes and they have a larger brain. You can tell pretty quick if a horse is getting the message. I have tried to get our people to understand that it isn't getting on the horse that counts, it's knowing when to get off. And if you can teach a trainer just to get on and just get the message across and get off, that's best.

Horses get bored. Now they won't if you take them out across country and let them see something new. But when you're sitting around here and going around the same track, they get very bored. This is where it's fallacy to say they're dumb animals because they get damn bored. They just don't think much of that. They do think a lot of going out on a trail, but you can find out awfully quick what their response is.

They'll do more for you with love and kindness. If I catch someone beating on a horse, they're not here anymore. I just won't allow it. I think you have to be smarter than the horse. If I catch them at it, and I've been fooled a time or two, but if I catch them beating on a horse they won't be here. That isn't to say you don't protect yourself from a young stud that's mad at you. You can't stand there and let him kill you and run over you. But if I catch them standing there beating on a horse, they won't be here. I won't permit it for one minute because there's no need to beat on a horse. You do it with kindness and love.

170

Horses of course understand people. They like some people, they dislike some, and Arabians respond better to kindness. I've seen it tried both ways. All you're doing when you're beating on a horse is you make him angry and you make him excited and he loses his temper. When you lose your own temper you don't reason very well, do you? Neither does a horse. He's upset. He's angry.

How did I learn all this? Maybe osmosis. I don't know. I've loved horses all my life. Every spare moment I had I went and spent time with them from when I was a little kid.

I brought a horse home one time when I was three or four years old. You could see all the bones in his body. My family almost died. But an old man had it and of course wanted to get rid of it, probably didn't have the money to feed it and I brought the horse home and begged and pleaded and kept it, put some feed in it. It was an ancient horse, it was old, it was skinny as a rail. But he looked gorgeous to me. Probably uglier than hell to anybody else. But I love horses and always have.

171

◆

Horses, you know, can be very loving, too. They come up and put their nose to you. They come stand next to you, want you to pet them. Or put their head on your shoulder. And very gently they put their head out to you. You know that when you're around them.

A lot of people make the mistake of trying to correct a horse by hitting them on the head. That should never be done. Then they get head shy and you can't do anything with them. Even if you hit them lightly you should never hit a horse on the head. No more than you should slap your children on the head because then they're afraid of you. If your hand goes up, they're afraid you're going to hit them on the head. You pat them on the neck or on the side of the head, but never go up.

Put your hand out and let them smell you. Horses are like us. They like certain people and they don't like certain others. Generally, they like ladies better than they do men because they're gentler.

◆

Somebody asked me once, you like horses more than jewelry? And the answer is yes, yes. They're living, vital things. And I love jewelry, remember, but horses can become like your children and they're so faithful and they're so good. Yes, I like them better than anything.

◆

Dr. Khristina Kirkland-West (veterinarian and general manager of the Chauncey Scottsdale ranch): Animals are ultimately sincere. They're ultimately honest. They are true. They're loyal. And they're very affectionate. They return affection and they return affection honestly. They return affection because they truly love you. They don't have many ulterior motives, especially with Mr. Chauncey. He's got horses on this ranch who know him individually and nicker to him. He doesn't feed these animals. He doesn't groom them. He doesn't bathe them or curry them. I think there's something very sincere and very honest about it that he likes.

◆

Jack Leonard (former *Time-Life* executive; U.S. Navy Commander, World War II; part-owner, Equestrian Manor before Chauncey and KOOL bought it; Irish bon vivant, and long-time personal friend): One story about a horse Tom sold. It was to a doctor that lived at Equestrian Manor and he wanted to buy a horse. He was a great guy, Dr. DeGrazia, and I told him, I said, Tom's got a great mare. Perfect for you. Let's go see it. So we went up and Tom showed him the horse and Dr. DeGrazia bought the horse. It was a good horse, $20,000. And he had the cash. And he says to Tom, will you take cash? Tom said, yeah. He had a white linen coat on, and he took the money and put it in both pockets of the white linen coat.

The next morning he had an eight o'clock barber's appointment and he took the white linen coat and put it on and it must of been 100 degrees, and he got into the barber's chair, he kept his coat on, and the barber put the towel and the sheet over him. And he kept saying, Tom, it's hot in here. Don't you want to take your coat off?

No, that's all right. I'll keep the coat on.

172

He's sitting there, it's at least 100 degrees at eight in the morning getting his hair cut and he's got the money in his pocket and won't take the coat off to hang it up. You know, the bank didn't open until nine so he couldn't make the deposit.

If he said it once he must of said twenty times, Tom, it's awful hot. Why don't you take your coat off? That barber still must think he's nuts.

♦

Tom Chauncey: How do you determine the price of a horse? You look at him. It's a judgment call that you make. It costs the same to produce a cheap horse as it does a good horse. It costs the same to feed him. You may not spend as much caring for him or her, but at this point in time, the horse needs to be healthy, of course. They have to be beautiful. They have to have class. Charisma. It's more like you'd say you pick out a Jimmy Stewart, or a Clark Gable. There are horses of that caliber. Or a Dottie Lamour or a Grace Kelly. There are horses that are in that class. They have the physique and the beauty to go with it. And when they have that, if they have the bloodlines and they're capable to reproduce, then they're worth a lot of money.

173

The horses that we read about are the exceptional ones, they're like the Clark Gables and the Swayzes, Walter Cronkites, they're exceptional horses. Everybody forgets that these high-priced horses are probably the best horses in the world. When you have the Saudi Arabians, from the cradle of Arabian horses before Christ, come here and buy horses, you know that you've got something special. And I've sent six horses over there.

On this farm at any given time, there are probably more great horses than there are anywhere else in the world. A few years ago, there's no question that there were more great horses in Arizona than anywhere else. Tucson and Phoenix. And some in Bisbee. There's some great horses in Arizona. And California has more.

I didn't start the Arabian industry, somebody started it thousands of years ago, but I may have given it its modern push. That's because I paid so much for Naborr. That made history all over the world, including Poland, including Russia. Nobody thought anybody in the world could get that horse out of Poland. But Mrs. McCormick did when he was fifteen. He was nineteen when I got him. And that made world history in the Arabian horse business.

I doubt if you'd pay that much today for a nineteen-year-old. You might for some of the rare ones, yes, for a great horse. Bask at that age was worth that much or more. Probably both of them not this year but two years ago, would have been worth five or six million, ten million dollars apiece because they produce that much in breedings.

◆

I told you Dr. Khris is a genius. Get her to tell you about Euros and also her embryo transplants.

Dr. Khris: Euros came here sterile. It was known in Europe that he was sterile and Mr. Chauncey loved the horse and wanted to try him anyway. Basically, the knowledge was there that a large number of horses who are on the track and who are being stressed heavily in athletic workouts, much like human beings, are not very fertile. And Mr. Chauncey was hoping that that was having a very bad effect on him, though we did not have the opportunity to examine him in Poland or to run any tests. So we really had no idea what was wrong with him when we brought him in.

He came here in January of 1985 and on Mr. Chauncey's birthday, which was January 20th, I thought I'd be real slick. We'd never collected the horse and we'd agreed that we'd give him a few days to calm down and mellow out a little bit before we collected him. And I thought, well this is a good opportunity.

Mr. Chauncey always rests from one until three in the afternoon so you've got a little time there where I felt like I could go out and collect the horse.

If the horse is fertile, I'll tell him we've got a breeding stallion. I'll take all the pressure off. Have a wonderful birthday present for him. If the horse isn't fertile I'll just keep my mouth shut and won't do anything for six weeks and see what we can come up with.

We literally waited until about 1:30 p.m. and we put mares in the barn; we went and collected the stallion, and I always take the collections back to the lab and look at them under the microscope. I threw a slide under the microscope, and it's very quiet in that lab and I never heard anything, and I looked up from the scope which was full of dead sperm, an entirely dead collection. And I turned around and Mr. Chauncey was standing right behind me at about 2:15 in the afternoon. He wanted to know what I was looking at and so I immediately told him.

Something he cannot tolerate is dishonesty in any form, so I immediately told him that it was a Euros collection and that I had just hoped that if it was normal I could give him a very good birthday present. But I let him look under the microscope and it was all dead. And it took us about ten weeks to get the horse breeding and get the horse to fertilize his mares and actually achieve some pregnancies.

We did it by basically changing everything we had for him. We altered his nutritional status. And frequent collections. Some horses are known as accumulators and they don't masturbate, and this horse was one of them. He needed to be collected so we were collecting him daily through this time. After about six weeks of collections, we started to get some motility and then by eight weeks we were getting good motility. It was a combination of exercise, nutrition and handling. We had only one young lady who handled him. Nobody else was allowed to groom him, touch him, wash him, bathe him, change him, whatever. So we felt that psychologically we had him under control. And then the frequent collections make a very big difference with this horse.

At that time too we had a student who was doing an externship here with us while getting his master's degree from Texas A & M in equine reproductive physiology, Jim Reed. He's gone on to be a manager at a very big farm in Texas. Texas A & M had an experimental semen extender at this time that they were putting horse semen in, and extenders up until that time had just been designed to keep semen alive. They hadn't been designed to enhance anything. And this one from Texas A & M claimed to enhance motility and enhance longevity.

So through Jim Reed we got hold of some of this and we started using it on the horse. I don't know that it made the difference in the horse, but I think it allowed us to start breeding

175

maybe two or three months earlier than if we hadn't had this extender.

He bred that very first year. In 1985, he bred seventy-six mares and achieved sixty-nine pregnancies out of that, so there were only seven of those mares that didn't get pregnant. It was about a 90 percent conception rate, which was wonderful. And he's been well over 90 percent each year after that. So he's been as fertile or more fertile than any other stallion on this ranch, or anywhere else in the United States.

The Polish people could not believe that we got him going. I think if the Poles had known that we could get him to be a breeding stallion, they would not have sold him. They did not believe us until we had babies on the ground that we had actually got him going. They were very surprised.

And we felt great relief. I couldn't imagine anything more awful than having that big gorgeous stallion out in the barn and not being able to get any children. It was a very big sigh of relief.

Earlier, I had advised Mr. Chauncey not to buy Euros. I was dead set against the purchase of the horse. It was common knowledge in the industry that the horse was sterile. He had been announced sterile at the Polish sale that previous September. I had no reason to believe whatsoever that this horse would ever breed or would ever be a fertile breeding stallion. Based on that I could not advise him to buy a horse who could not breed. And then to have to pay cash with no warranty of fertility. It was written right on the contract that they would not warrant him for fertility. That is if he got him over here and he was a very expensive gelding, then that's all we had, a very expensive gelding.

Of the comparable cases in this country, or anywhere in the world, for that matter, Secretariat is probably the most famous. Secretariat came off the track and had an exceedingly difficult time his first year in the breeding shed, getting his mares in foal, and it even made some national press that Secretariat might be a flop as a stallion. Again, it was extreme athletic stress. It took them about six months and they got him going and he's a very strong breeding stallion now. That's probably the most famous. But it's not that uncommon to take breeding stallions, or mares for that matter, off the track and out of rigorous athletic training and have a decrease in fertility for a period of time.

◆

Embryo transfer technology was available back in 1982 and 1983. It started being done on ranches in 1984 and we started it in 1986. We've had six mares enrolled in that program and we've had four successful transfers. So we've got four babies being produced. It's not wide-scale, and the success rate is still much less than that of allowing a mare to have her own baby.

The embryo transfer procedure was designed for a mare who either could not carry her own pregnancy or who for reasons of going to a horse show or being too young, the owners didn't want her to carry her own pregnancy. So we actually breed a mare who is in heat, that's called the donor mare, and she provides one half of the genetic material. And the stallion we're breeding to her provides the other half of the genetic material. And we breed her until we believe we have an ovulation and a conception. Then on day seven of what would be her pregnancy, when we have a seven day-old embryo present, we flush that embryo from the donor mare and surgically place it into a third party mare. She is really a surrogate mare or just acting as an incubator so that she does then carry the pregnancy, give birth to the foal, nurse it and raise it, but makes no genetic contribution to the foal.

The flushing is a non-surgical flushing technique that's done through the vagina and cervix with a liter-in flush and a liter-out flush with a cell culture medium, and we actually have filters that are of such a size that we can catch the embryo and then we scan under a magnifying microscope to locate it. Not everywhere tries embryo transfers. It requires a certain skill level. It's labor intensive. It requires a good number of people and it's expensive. You have to have the caliber of horse that warrants doing it. You wouldn't do it for a $1,000 - $2,000 horse. You save it for horses that have a great deal of value and gene pools that are very valuable to the breed registries.

◆

Tom Chauncey: We have two ranches at Winslow and they run about 160,000 acres, the two of them, and it's about 200 miles around them. Each has a huge mountain in its center and there's a highway that goes in between them. Coming out of Winslow, you go south about nine miles. The headquarters for one is on the left and the other is on the right. One is West Clear Creek Ranch and the other is East Clear Creek Ranch. The meteor crater up there used to be part of the ranch before they made it a national park. It's all beautiful, big open country, well-watered and very beautiful, one of the best cattle ranches in the United States.

178   Another ranch, 100 miles from there, was the old John Wayne ranch. That is the 26 Bar Ranch, and we raise mostly cattle up there. The three ranches will run about 300,000 head of cattle. The Wayne ranch has the Little Colorado head waters going right through the middle of it and in the meadows right in front of the house, it's about 6,800-7,000 feet high. This is five minutes from the airport. You can land and within minutes you're right on the house. Go up the hill and it's seven miles and you're at 9,000-10,000 feet. We can't even get up there ourselves in the winter. The snow is too high, several feet high.

◆

Marge Injasoulian: While he was at KOOL, Tom bought a ranch up in Mayer called H Lazy A. It was a 10,000-acre place for him to go to because he never got away.

He never took a vacation, nothing, ever. Vacations were just not his cup of tea. But finally when he bought the H Lazy A ranch he managed to spend the summers up there but it didn't matter because that was his summer office. We'd all go traipsing up there and I'd go up there with my campaigns and it was just like he was in the office. At any rate, that's where he really got to like farming and horses and Herefords.

◆

Tom Chauncey: I get up early so it may be by five in the morning the phone starts ringing, and it's a fellow from the ranch about some cattle. It's an easy time to decide what we're going to do with the cattle, when we're going to move them, when we're going to brand them, are we going to sell any of them, how are we going to breed them, which ones we'll keep in the herd, which ones we won't keep, which ones we will register, which ones we won't.

We have two herds. One is primarily of the John Wayne cattle breedings and some Kenny Rogers cattle. Generally, those cattle, or a number of them, we register. They're purebreds. The others we put into the herd.

Those decisions and others. Irrigation problems, when we go from one ranch to the other, whether they go up on the mountains early or late. We'll move 2,000 or more head of cattle in the next couple of months, either by driving them or hauling them. And of course we're branding, doctoring, vaccinating.

I got mixed up with cattle because there were in Arizona when I was a kid what we called the three Cs — cattle, cotton, copper. They were the industries. And of course living in this kind of a country, I always loved cattle, loved horses. Particularly, I had an ongoing great love for purebred and commercial Hereford cattle. I guess I like cattle as much as horses but it's a different thing. You try not to get too attached to any of them, but you do and that's awfully hard when you sell them (and you do have to sell them to stay in business).

I get pretty attached to animals. I always have. They get attached to people. They know you and they know who likes them. I don't buy this thing that they're dumb animals. They're not dumb animals. They're smarter than we are. They've learned how to exist for centuries. Cattle aren't as smart as the horse but they're certainly smart enough to know how to live, how to survive out in the open. In that way they may be even smarter.

For instance, Battle Domino was a huge bull that was gentle and the kids used to ride. He would go wherever the kids would go. A huge bull. He liked the kids. The kids would ride him and he'd swing his head, but they'd close the gate behind him and Battle Domino would go up and he'd put the gate in his horns and throw it about thirty feet out in the air and walk through it.

He had our handyman running around with a cart and an extra gate all the time. If Battle Domino wanted to get over where the kids were, gates never bothered him. He just threw them out of the way. The man wanted to kill him. He was screaming and hollering. But to be prepared he always had a hammer and a spare gate.

◆

The North Scottsdale ranch is 160 acres, a half-mile square, all pasture except where there's buildings. Probably 300 horses right now, most of them mine.

I bought this place originally for a place for those towers. I had to have it for the geographic location for the radio towers, back in the 1960s.

The thing that has now made this land so valuable is the Princess Hotel across the road and down a mile. When that started showing out of the ground, all of a sudden, everybody started wanting this land. The hotel made it worth a lot of money.

This was the old Brown Land and Cattle Company. All the way into Brown Street. If it hadn't been for needing those towers, I wouldn't have come out here and bought. I don't know why I bought the whole 160 acres. Sometimes it was hard to handle and keep, to pay for. Even as cheap as it was, and it was very cheap, 4 ½ percent interest.

Chapter 12

Bypass

Ed Diethrich came to Phoenix to open a heart institute, and there was a fellow in broadcasting named Mark Austad Evans, who was ambassador to Finland and Norway. He kept saying, Tom, there's a doctor coming to town. He's delightful, he's wonderful. And Mark had a heart thing. And he said, I'd wish you'd be on his board. I said, I'm on forty boards now. I just can't get on. He said, but you'd like this man and this is needed here. And he brought me a book to read and he kept after me and after me and finally I met Dr. Diethrich and I liked him. So he said, will you come on the board and help us? I was just freshly off the board of the Barrow Neurological Institute so I said, okay.

One night we were sitting and talking at St. Joseph's Hospital after a Heart Institute board meeting was over and Dr. Diethrich looked over and he said, Tom, do you feel all right?

I'm fine.

No you aren't. What's wrong?

I'm tired.

Just for the heck of it, why don't we check you?

Well, he did. The next thing you know they've got me on that thing upside down where they put the dye in and you can see it too. They showed me the occlusions. Mostly closed, three arteries. Triple. I had to have a triple bypass.

He says, number one, you've got to quit smoking. And if you want to live, you better get this bypass.

I want to think about it.

No. I'm telling you, you don't have much time to fool around. This is serious. You've got to get that blood moving around.

So I decided, okay, I'd do it. I went in and he came in that night and also Dr. Kinard, who was one of his associates, and I usually had two pockets of cigarettes, I wouldn't buy a shirt without two pockets, and I also had a pack on the table.

Now, he said, this is what I want to talk to you about. He took the package. I wish we could open you up and show you. Your chest is like charcoal and it won't work. And he says, if you continue to smoke you might as well forget this operation. You're going to be dead. You better quit.

I took the cigarettes and I laid them there, that night. After he left I started to smoke one, then I put it out. Okay. So I threw them in the wastebasket and I haven't smoked since.

I discovered you're awfully sick after that operation. First of all, they cut you from up here under your chin all the way down, then they crack you open and take your heart out. And the thing that makes Dr. Diethrich great, they tell me, is he has the heart back going very fast. They call him fast fingers. Less than an hour, I think, he had my heart back. They strip an artery out of this leg and one out of this leg and in little over an hour I was back together, back on the heart. The shorter time you're on the support system, the shorter your recovery.

My problem was that I just couldn't get up and walk. Finally, I got them to let me come home. It was twenty-five miles down to the hospital where he was, and as busy as he was, he'd come out there and he'd say, get out of bed. We're going to walk. Walk hell. I can't even get up.

Yes, you can.

And he'd take me up these roads, faster, faster. And he did it until he got me better. He said, now you keep this up. Every day. He'd call and check on me. That's the kind of guy he is. It's amazing that he could get out of the hospital. He's very busy.

My family, there isn't a person alive. Eight children and my Mother and Father, they're all dead. I suppose if they would have had the same opportunity and known Ed Diethrich, they'd all have lived longer. The only reason I knew him is I was on his board. You would have never gotten me to go see a doctor. I never had a checkup. I didn't believe in it. I was too busy.

But I'm also convinced I wouldn't be here today if I hadn't been on that board.

Chapter 13

What Others Say

Homer Lane: How do you describe Tom Chauncey? He has always been volatile, mercurial, but he'd come down just as fast as he'd go up. You could really screw up at KOOL and it was almost impossible to get fired unless you lied to him. If you lied to him or made a mistake and tried to cover it up, you were history. You were just plain history. But if you came to him and said, Tom, I really screwed this up. He'd say, okay, how do you suggest we fix it? Or make a suggestion to fix it and go on. It's past. Go on to something else. That's just the way he was. Just go on to something else. Put that behind us and move ahead. But if you were devious, he didn't have time for devious people. We all worked too hard for that. Didn't have time for that. Wouldn't put up with it. Honesty is a word that is synonymous with Tom Chauncey.

Too, he's a guy whose word is it. If he tells you something you can go to the bank and draw money on it.

He saw the beginning. He was here when Arizona came of age. And he's seen it all happen, but he's done more than see it happen, he's helped to make it happen, all the way along the line.

◆

Bill Lester: I would say he's a loyal, fun Irishman and to people who said, boy he has a hot temper, I'd say, yeah, but on the other hand let me tell you something. If you were in a bar fight and he was at your back, you wouldn't even have to turn around. You see? So I'm talking about loyalty, depth, compassion. I think he's very Irish in his loyalties and his affection for people. Very affectionate person. Has high standards.

♦

Bill Close: He's a no-nonsense, no-bull guy with a tremendous sense of humor. He is also a very caring person. I know of at least three occasions when people on the staff had a problem that money would help solve, and he authorized a check for $1,000 to each individual.

You've heard the old expression that as you go through life, do what needs to be done and don't worry who gets the credit. That's Tom Chauncey. Things needed to be done and he didn't want any credit. He didn't worry about who gets the credit. He just flat didn't want the credit. He is a doer. He is a shaker. He is a mover. Other than my dad, he is one of the two men who have had the most influence on my life.

To see him day in and day out, you would not realize that he walks with kings. He doesn't put on airs. He's as plain and simple and as straightforward as an arrow.

I recall the end of something that had bothered Tom for a long time. That is, a challenge was filed against our license and among those who were filing was Harry Rosenzweig, the longstanding pillar and statesman of the Republican party. Boyhood chum of Barry Goldwater.

One day Harry Rosenzweig called me, I guess he was too embarrassed to call Tom, and said, Bill, I've got a piece of paper here and it says we're withdrawing our application, claim, our cross filing for your TV channel. I went in to call Tom. He never went out to lunch. He always had Audrey run out and get him soup or a sandwich. And I said, I got good news. I just heard from Harry and he's withdrawing. It was just a one paragraph release.

He was excited as a kid, a little girl getting her first doll, and he said, call a staff meeting immediately. The whole staff. So I called around and everybody's out to lunch, but there were a few people. Called them in.

We met in Tom's spacious office and Tom said, Bill, read to them what you just read to me. So I did. And I think I added something like, boy, it's just like Christmas in September.

At that, Tom said to our comptroller, write everybody a check for $100.

And Jerry said, you can't do that.

Why can't I?

Jerry explained that the IRS had frozen the number of bonuses you could give and it was traditional to give a Christmas bonus and so he said, you can only give one bonus per year.

Notwithstanding, bonuses were handed out. And we had a staff in excess of 200. That's $20,000. And when it came to Christmas time, we got our Christmas bonus, too.

◆

At one time or another, everybody who worked at KOOL hated his guts. But only momentarily. I don't think that anybody ever hated his guts on this staff other than saying, that white-haired old son of a bitch, and then five minutes later, you know, he's a heck of a guy. I don't think anybody on the staff ever hated him. We used to bitch and moan all the time because we couldn't do something, but we'd get our answer right away. For example, I wanted to get a Western Union clock in the news-room. And what was the rental fee? Two dollars fifty cents a month. I talked to Tom about it every once in a while and he said, no, no. And then one day he called me over to the office on the patio out here and said, Bill, what do you think of this, and handed me some keys. He gave me keys to a new car to drive.

I said, you son of a buck, you won't give me a clock but you'll give me a new car to drive and I don't need the car, but I need the clock. He said, that's the way I can afford the car. A prince of a guy.

When the company sold, he gave Mary Jo West and me, each of us, for $1, a Cadillac Seville that he had bought for us to drive. (Of course, the new owners came along and put on my income tax the book value of the car, so I had to pay income tax on $17,000, $18,000, $20,000, something like that. But Tom had made his point.)

◆

Jack Leonard: He's a character, a good character. He's got a lot of pizzazz. He's a good businessman. He's shrewd.

And he certainly knows how to turn a dollar. But at the same time, he's been very charitable. He came into this town with nothing. He made his mark. He's been a great influence on the growth of this town. And he's been a great contributor. He has done a lot of good work for people. He's done a lot of good work that people don't know about.

He's easy to know. In a crowd you'll know him because of his characteristics, his looks and everything, his white hair. He knows his way around and he's got good basic street-sense. He knows how to work with people. He knows a lot of people. He's one of the better known Phoenicians who has never held public office. He's helped a lot of people attain a lot of success. If you met him at a party, you'd remember him. He's gregarious. He's friendly. He's sharp. He knows how to mix with people. He knows how to get to the heart of things. He's never fazed by work.

He stayed as one of the people; he was never a big-shot. He was as friendly with the people who worked around the ranch, or horse people, the man on the street as he was with his friendly bankers. In other words, he knew his barber, he knew his shoe-shine guy and he knew the chairman of the board of the companies. He could talk to a horse trainer or a stableboy as well as bankers, lawyers, or the governor. That's what made him really a force in town.

And his willingness to cooperate and turn out for any event that he could for the community. He put back into the community an awful lot for what he got out of it. So he's rubbed elbows with the small man, the middle man, and the top man and he's kept his feet on the ground and remembers where he came from.

He never ran for office because he never wanted to be beholden to people as a political servant. He served the community well assisting people, but I don't think he ever wanted to take the baton himself and run with it. He wouldn't flow with the crowd because if he has an opinion, he sticks to it and he's been able to stick to his opinion because he didn't have to be influenced.

He wouldn't walk away from a political issue. If he believed in something and he was standing in a group of ten people, and nine of them thought differently, I think he would express his opinion. And I don't think politically you can think that way. To sum it up, he was the most un-pompous person I ever knew.

◆

Dr. Khris: Mr. Chauncey is absolutely unique. He is absolutely generous and fair. He's got both feet on the ground. He is a self-made man so he understands both having and not having. He understands the importance of generosity at the right times and the importance of encouraging people at the right time. He is extremely demanding and believes in dealing with the bottom line.

If I want to discuss a subject with him, if I can't state my case in twenty-five words or less, I've lost him. He wants bottom line. Constantly, constantly bottom line. No powder, no puff, no smoke. Just tell him what's going on and we'll move on to another subject. That's made him extremely efficient throughout the years.

He's extremely many-faceted. He's got a wide variety of personality traits and attributes and he is a very good man to work for and a very fair man to work for. But at the same time a very demanding man, demanding of himself and demanding of those around him. He is certainly demanding of someone being conscientious in their work. Somebody being dedicated to their work without any constraints by time or days.

He absolutely insists that people who work for him work hard and work diligently. He tolerates nothing short of that. If that includes the middle of the night, so what? If the job needs to be done, the job needs to be done.

He says I'm here too much, but being a resident veterinarian on a farm that's got 250 horses is like having 250 children, and horses are around-the-clock work. They're seven days a week, twenty-four hours a day, and they can get sick at any time or give birth at any time or get injured at any time.

Mr. Chauncey also is very diverse in his likes. He is a lover of the arts. A lover of beautiful things. Anything that's aesthetically pleasing, his art work and his bronzes and those things that he surrounds himself with. There's everything in here from antique to current to Western art to Middle Eastern art to Far Eastern art. You know, he just likes what he likes. Self-made man. Very intelligent man. Very hard-working man. Very perceptive man.

He's extremely good at meeting someone for the first time and getting a feel for whether he can trust that person or whether that person is a good person and somebody he wants to do business with or not. Very intuitive.

I wouldn't call him a horse trader. I'd say he's a horse collector. I don't think he'd ever sell one if he didn't have to. If he were living in his own perfect world, he'd have as many horses as he wanted and if that was a thousand, it would be a thousand. The horses that have been sold in the auctions here are almost always by necessity where we've gotten too many. He doesn't like selling them. He just likes having them. Having them around. He likes being able to see them. Every Sunday at our public showing he sees forty or fifty. During the week it's not uncommon for him to walk the barns and walk the pastures and we try to show him every horse on the ranch at least twice a year. He probably sees about 100 horses a week.

Many other people can talk about him, but you can put all of us together and all of our comments together and you still won't know everything there is to know about him. He has many facets and he's very complex, and he can still be quite unpredictable. There's just a whole lot to the man. I don't know anybody that's got him figured out. He is his own man.

On any subject, on any given topic of discussion, on any problem that comes up on the ranch, I might think I know what he's going to say or what he's going to do or how he's going to behave, and about half the time I'm not right. He deals with every situation individually and he's extremely self-motivated and self-confident. Obviously, he has a very diverse background. I'm sure that contributes to it.

You've got your work cut out for you to try to paint a picture of this man because he is extremely deep. There's a lot there. He defies description and he defies explanation.

♦

188

Jack Leonard: Naborr and Chauncey became a love affair. You'd see him go out to that barn every morning and talk to that horse like he was talking to you, and bring him his fresh carrots and feed him. It was a daily routine, his love for that horse. Naborr, you could see, when Tom came on the ranch, Naborr would start prancing back and forth in the stall. Many a time I went out and fed Naborr carrots with him and Naborr could hear his step coming. There would be all kinds of other attendants around there, but when Tom would start coming his way, Naborr got all excited in the stall.

◆

Bill Lester: Over the years I find out a lot of stories about Mr. C.

I found out about a little church school on the South side, when Tom visited one day, the black minister who came out and just really embraced Tom, and pointed over to a school bus over there that Tom had purchased for them without anybody knowing it and giving it to them. I would have never known it, except this guy in front of me saying, Tom, that's been the greatest thing.

Another one:

We're sitting around the table at the station and Bill Close is the VP for news. We're all around the conference table and Tom stops everything and says, hey, wait a minute. Willie, Close, who's this girl that you had do a piece the other night and her eyes are kind of cockeyed?

Close said, that's so-and-so.

What's the matter with her eyes?

Oh, I think it's from her childhood, Tom.

Can they be straightened?

Well, I don't know.

Why don't you find out? She's not a bad-looking girl, is she?

No.

Isn't she a hard worker?

Oh, she's one of the best we have.

Well, find out.

When Close came back he said it would cost a lot of money, that's why she never did it, she never had the money to do this.

And Tom said, well don't you think we ought to do it?

That was the end of that. They did.

Still one more:

In Phoenix they got a group of people together to form a deal and get this thing going where the cities would get money every place they could and would move into the poverty areas and give them all the services available. The planning was wonderful. Everybody sat around and said this is going to be the greatest thing that anybody in the world's ever done. And finally, Tom was there with the others, a business person and quick moving, no question. And you can just hear Tom:

Well now, where are we? What are we doing? What's the next step here?

And somebody said, the trouble is we can't get any seed money. Everything from the government is seed money, you know. Can't get any seed money so this is as far as we can go until something happens in Washington. If they can send us some money we'll get going.

And Tom said quickly, how much money you talking to get started here?

Oh, I think we'd have to get at least $25,000. That was a lot of money then.

Tom said, well, Herman and I will put up the $25,000, won't we Herman? So let's get going.

That was the start of LEAP in Phoenix. When Herman Chanen told me the story he laughed and said, well you know I'd do anything Chauncey says. They have some kind of a friendship that is just wonderful. They're partners in businesses and such things.

But Herman then said, I went home and worried about what should we call this thing? There ought to be a good name for it that would have good visibility. One night about 1 a.m. I woke up and I thought, LEAP. Leadership, Education and Advancement for Phoenix. That'll be wonderful. And he said, I dialed Tom. Hello.

This is Herman, Tom, and I have a great idea.

It better be a blankety-blanking good one. Do you know what time it is, Herman? One a.m.

And so he told Tom it was LEAP and that's what was used for many, many years.

LEAP. I don't know if you know how huge it is in Phoenix. If you look in the phone book and see all the offices, all the things they do, you'll know. It was the original city commission to help the disadvantaged with housing, education, jobs.

◆

Jack Leonard: Did he ever mention Odyssey III? No, he probably wouldn't.

It's a 92-foot motor yacht and it's got all the facilities. It has a main cabin and two other staterooms. Up forward you can sleep up to six crew members. It's a Choy Lee boat, built in China, he's a famous boat builder over there. It's fiberglass and has twin GM 750 diesels with every up-to-date navigational aid. You can pilot it from three stations — the main deck, the flying bridge and then on top of that there's a third station that you use basically for visibility or for backing into a port. You could go in it from here to Europe without too much trouble. It has a cruising range of about 4,000 miles. It's equipped to go to sea.

When he had it, it went out of the harbor twice and one of those times he wasn't on it. He sent some of his friends over and we took them out for a cruise. But when Tom was on it, we didn't go outside the harbor. He had some friends he wanted to cruise around and show them San Diego bay. Now it's been sold.

◆

Herman Chanen (Chairman of the Board, President and CEO, Chanen Construction Company; former chair, Phoenix 40; 1988-89 President, Arizona Board of Regents): It was back in the 1960s when I was chairing the United Way that I first met Tom Chauncey. At that time, it was called the United Fund and the goal for that year was $1,726,696, a 26 percent increase over the prior year.

I had a dynamite team consisting of people like Gene Pulliam, Publisher of the *Arizona Republic* and *Phoenix Gazette*; Walter Bimson, Chairman of the Board of Valley National Bank; Walt Lucking, President of Arizona Public Service, and Frank Snell, a founder of the law firm of Snell & Wilmer. All of those people worked their tails off and about ten days before the drive was scheduled to end, we were still approximately $125,000 short of reaching our goal.

I can remember Gene Pulliam saying to me, our campaign team has done a good job, we've achieved more than a 15 percent increase over last year and it's now time to wrap it up. But I just didn't want to quit.

192

I had heard the name Tom Chauncey numerous times, but had never met the man. Someone told me that if I needed some help or advice, see Tom Chauncey. So I did. I called his office at KOOL and made an appointment with him.

That first meeting was the beginning of our friendship. He called Jim Patrick who was President of Valley National Bank, after which we went to Jim's office and spent the better part of three days and three nights making telephone calls, and as a result, raised the last $125,000. I still have the scrapbook with all of the hand-written notes showing how the money was raised with $500 and $1,000 pledges until we reached our goal. Those days were pretty exciting.

What Tom did was to call people that had already given and got them to increase their pledges. In some cases, he called people that had never supported the United Fund in the past. And what was amazing was that he didn't do any high-pressure selling. He would just call up and say, Mr. Smith, this is Tom Chauncey. I need your help. And almost every time they'd say, Tom, you've got it. What do you need? Absolutely amazing.

He's still the same way. I can't remember when I have ever heard anyone turn Tom down for anything. Tom is the kind of person that wouldn't ask someone to do something for a cause if he felt that he was imposing on them or if it would be difficult for them to say no.

That's how I met Tom. And it was love at first sight. Since that time, we've been involved in many community projects together. And there is no question about it, he is my best friend. He always will be.

There is a lot of magic in Tom. That is the best way I can describe him.

Everything he touches is like touching magic. He is tough, gentle, persevering, kind, modest — all at the same time. He does so much for so many people. Most of the time they don't even know Tom is involved.

Over the years our friendship continued to grow. There are months at a time that we never see each other, or even talk, but we are always there for each other, if needed.

Hanging on the wall in my office is a civic power of attorney that I gave to Tom back in the early 1960s. It was witnessed by Paul Fannin, Governor of Arizona at the time. It gave Tom authority to commit me to various civic endeavors. Various people would call and tell me to send them a check based on some pledge or commitment Tom had made on my behalf, using my power of attorney. I always sent the check and never asked any questions. I do the same thing to him and he has always come through.

The year that I chaired the United Fund drive was the year that we started the Tom Chauncey Award in honor of Tom. It is given to the outstanding volunteer of the year and, of course, Tom received it for his efforts during the year that I was chairman.

After we reached our goal, we decided that we wanted to give Tom something special and we ultimately wound up buying a huge silver trophy that was originally made that year for the Rose Bowl. Tom still has that trophy in his home.

◆

Tom Chauncey: Well, getting that money was just good luck and hard work. A lot of very generous people gave me a lot of money. It wasn't that tough, it was just work.

The way he got that trophy was something. He went to the Dodge Trophy Factory and there was this beautiful bowl that sits out here now, with roses all over it. He said, we sure like that. But Ray Dodge said, no way. That's the Tournament of Roses, that's for the Rose Bowl.

Well, we'd sure like to have it. Tom Chauncey really should get something.

He said, who?

Tom Chauncey is the man that we want to present this to.

He said, I've known Tom for a long time. We've been friends for quite a while and he helped me with some business years ago. If you want that trophy you can have it for him. I'll make another one.

I had known Ray Dodge when he was having a hard time selling trophies in Arizona. He had a new idea and a good one and I introduced him to some people and opened some doors for him. Schools, I think. And also I took his line on. I didn't do that much. Just what you normally do when people come to town, they just want a friend.

♦

Herman Chanen: I guess the best way I could describe Tom is to say that he is honest, loyal, gentle, tough, smart, stimulating, very creative — a lot of contrast. He is exciting to be around and to watch run his business. The people that work for him respect him and love him.

Let me tell you about a running duel that Tom and I had over the years, until we called a truce. When I first met Tom, I learned that one thing he disliked most was to have his birthday acknowledged. So I started doing things like renting a huge billboard and parking it on a trailer in front of his home or flying huge gas-filled barrage balloons in his front yard with "Happy Birthday, Tom" written on them, or renting an airplane with flashing lights to wish Tom a Happy Birthday as it flew across northern Arizona over Tom's ranch. Of course, Tom was not to be outdone. I remember waking up one morning on my birthday (a week after his) and finding my entire lawn covered with hundreds of pink balloons. I guess there was a lot of boy in both of us. We really did some outrageous things to each other.

♦

Marge Injasoulian: He built his reputation over the years on honesty and quality merchandise. If you take a look at those two things, honesty and quality merchandise, he did the same thing in the broadcast industry and the same thing with the Arabian horses. Those two principles have always been very important to him. He always dealt very honestly with people and he always had quality merchandise to trade.

◆

Bill Miller: Tom Chauncey is bigger than life. Incredibly intelligent. Fantastic memory. A true pioneer. An enormous amount of personal resources within the community and within the nation. If you needed information on something or you needed help on something, he knew the best people in the world on that thing. If a friend needed a heart operation, he knew the best doctor in the world. If you needed to know something about television news, he knew on a very intimate basis the people who were the very best and most respected news people in the world. He was able to link into that for you.

195

He was immensely powerful to the people who were around him. He ran things pretty much with an iron hand. And yet, at the same time, during the times I worked with him, he deserved the iron hand. He was smarter than anybody. I didn't see him make many mistakes.

He was one of these guys that you'd hand a memo to and he would read that memo and a year later he would quote you a figure off of that memo. And he hadn't seen it in a year. He had that ability. There was something uncanny about his intellect and about his memory. It was very, very good. So when he tied those two things together, this incredible memory and this great intellect, he could shoot through a whole bunch of things right to the core of a subject or problem.

He could sight the direction of where he was going, shoot right through to where the meaning was, and get at the core. Whatever it was. Whether it was a problem or a project or a dream. He could pass up all the baloney and get right to the important facts. I don't remember any meetings with him going more than a half hour, and he didn't like memos that were more than half a page. One page at the most.

When we came away from it, all of us that worked there, we said, you know, we learned a lot about broadcasting along the way, but more than that we learned about life.

He would say, here are the rules of good journalism:

Be fair. Be honest. Be as complete as possible. Be accurate.

And now to this day I believe those are the best rules of journalism. I learned that from him. I learned it at an early age. I never saw him condone anything that was dishonest. I think I learned a great deal of honesty from Tom Chauncey. And he would make the point many times. If we lose this account or ten accounts or 100 accounts, we're not going to do something that is dishonest. So that had a great impact on me.

He had a lot of respect for other people. He had a lot of respect for religion. I remember one time when we went to great lengths to remove a short scene from a documentary where a farmer was just so incensed with what was going on with water or something that he said God dammit. Tom Chauncey said, that line's going to have to come out. He said, that violates the First Commandment and I won't allow that on the air. Didn't mind bastard or son of a bitch, but God dammit couldn't go on. Those were his personal codes and we stuck by those, we lived by those.

We did a documentary once on the inner city, and we were shooting it at the Matthew-Henson housing project. One of the biggest problems for those people was cockroaches. They were just inundated with cockroaches. There were millions. You would walk into these places and there would be cockroaches everywhere. So we had one of the ladies capture some of these cockroaches from her kitchen for us and we took them into the studio and we shot very tight shots of them for impact so that when we did this story and the people talked about cockroaches, we would see these cockroaches that were from Matthew-Henson on the screen in giant form.

And he looked at that and he said, are these Matthew-Henson cockroaches?

Yes sir, they are.

Did you shoot them at Matthew-Henson?

No. We shot them here in the studio.

Doesn't look accurate to me.

So we went back and shot those cockroaches again, not the same ones, we found new ones, and we shot them as they existed at Matthew-Henson. He was one of those people who did not like to fake a thing. And I grew up that way. I grew up thinking you can't fake stuff on television and we just didn't do it when it was in television news. So those were lessons.

◆

He was like a father to me in the way that he taught me. My image of him was kind of fatherly. He was really tough. Frankly, I didn't talk back to him. In a lot of the same way that your relationship is with your Dad — you respect him, you like him, you have a lot of faith in him, and yet the way you treat him is more like a father, I think. And the way he treated me, I think, was probably more like a son.

197

For example:

My Grandfather was living in Florida and had a terrible stroke. My Father went down to see him and put him in the hospital. But my Dad called me and said, Son, I've got a real problem here. They don't have a hospital down here in St. Petersburg like Barrow where they can deal with this neurological problem that your Grandfather has. Could you look and see if there is some way, if it's possible, to get him to Phoenix? And I went and talked to Homer Lane and Homer went and talked to Tom Chauncey and Homer called me back and he said, be at Sky Harbor Airport at five o'clock tomorrow morning, there will be a plane waiting for you. And they flew me to Florida. I picked up my Grandfather and I brought him back here, put him in Barrow Neurological Institute where they were ready for him and Mr. Chauncey had made sure that he had the best neurosurgeon in America and that's the kind of things they did for me. I mean, they said, we want to do this for you. There are a lot of stories like that.

◆

Back in the early days when Mr. C had the H Lazy A ranch, he decided it would be a great idea to let the people at the station see this other life, cowboying. So once a year anybody who wanted to on their Saturday and Sunday could come up and be a cowboy for a couple of days. And he would provide everybody a horse and food, and the food was fantastic. I mean, you'd come back in off the range and there'd be this catered steak dinner with fresh shrimp cocktail and all the beer you could drink. It was an incredible experience for some of us because we really did round up the cattle and we really did do the dehorning and we really did all the corral work. We probably got in people's way more than we helped but we learned a lot. We learned a real respect for that kind of a life.

◆

He gave so much to this city and to those of us who had that opportunity to work with him. He's a unique person. He's one of a kind.

I've never met another Tom Chauncey.

Chapter 14

What
Tom Chauncey
Says

Nobody in this world ever had a really good life without the benefit and help of other people.

Throughout my lifetime there has always been somebody or a number of people who have helped me. Tremendous. Either with my grammar or my manners, my clothes, or whatever.

Mexican-Americans. Mexicans from Mexico. Blacks. Jewish people. Germans. Italians. You can learn something from all of them. You learn from people more than you do from books. It's amazing how many people are willing to help you if you let them. If you'll smile and be nice to people.

Success in business is very simple. Treat people right. Treat them honestly and you don't worry about the bottom line, the dollars, but if you treat them right, success will come.

More than anything else, I've always supported housing, equal rights, women, the whole bit. I believe in it strongly. You can't have a decent society with people hungry and poor. But you can't give it all to them, either. It would make bums out of them. So there's a fine line. Who decides that line, I don't know. I'm not smart enough.

But I do know they need housing and they need food and they don't need to be put in a bunch like a thousand people in one place out there and left out in the cold. Imagine how you and I'd be if we were suffering like that. Imagine if you and I were black how nasty we'd be trying to be equal. Blacks still are not treated fairly. They're treated better than they were, but we've got a long way to go. You can't live in a society where there are people hungry at night, kids aren't clothed. If you don't have a conscience about that, you've failed as a society.

That doesn't mean that people shouldn't work or help themselves. They ought to be proud of their accomplishments. I think most people really want to work. There are some that don't but most do. They just need to be given an opportunity, need somebody to open doors and help them.

You know, people who don't have a whole hell of a lot are the most compassionate. It's the poor who really take care of people. We get selfish and self-centered the more we acquire. And we have to guard against that if we're going to be decent human beings. But it's really the poor who care and the poor who give the most. I've worked on almost every drive to raise money for good causes in Phoenix since I was a child. I did it because I had to. I just was compelled to do it because people have been so good to me. I wouldn't have had anything to eat without people helping me. The clothes I wore came from other people. My shoes, too, for a long time. Generally, people who care enough can make the most difference. And that means us. We can't just sit here and be comfortable and everything, knowing that that's going on without at least trying. If we can't help financially, we can help with our presence.

◆

Happiness is not in the pocketbook. You lose sight of common decency and human beings and if you don't treat people as you'd like to be treated, you fail.

It's a simple life, really. Treat people like you'd like to be treated. A smile, a friendly handshake, and you can't fake that. If you treat people any other way, you're never going to be happy, you're going to be miserable. And you're going to make everybody around you miserable.

My brother said to me once, we were working on a picture, some people came up to him and said, George, we'd like to meet John Wayne. Of course, we're just little people and we'll never get the chance unless we can get someone big like you to introduce us. He looked at them and he said, you know, there are no little people. There are people. I don't know any little people and you're not little people. And if you'll meet me here tomorrow morning, so and so time, I'll see that you meet whoever you want to meet.

He always said, there are no little people. And there really aren't. They're people. You might get kicked in the teeth once in a while with your guard down, treating people nicely, but over the long span of life, you never regret kindnesses to people. You regret being nasty. You live with that. It's stressful. But there's nothing to regret about being nice to somebody. There's nothing to regret about a smile.

Without the interplay and the camaraderie and the things that go with people, we'd be nobody. I wouldn't be sitting here with all these things. For me, it was people.

201

◆

I don't know how in the world women who work, who have a drunken husband, can support their children. It's got to be a God-awful torture thing.

Women have to be awfully strong. Women are the ones that are crucial to this society. They're the glue. And I think women can hold any job that men can. I just don't believe, not for one minute, that women aren't smarter than men. If you don't think they're smarter, go to any grade school and ask the same question of the boys and girls to see who's the smartest.

Think about women. From the time they're a little girl, they're protecting themselves from some filthy guy who's trying to put his hands on them. They have to be coy without making waves. They learn it at a very early age. But think of a girl's life. Horrible men putting their hands all over them, or trying to. They have to protect themselves.

Women, they're smarter because they have to be. They have a tough time out in the business world. Especially now when they're all working together. But they're capable of handling it and will handle it. I don't think that we've begun to see the equality that should be and I think they've made great strides.

No one goes his way alone. We all need help from people. I think if there's one thing that makes both men and women better it's friends. Without them, you don't have much.

◆

One woman who is terribly important to me is Audrey Herring, who has been with me twenty-eight going on twenty-nine years. She's loyal. She's capable. She's absolutely honest. If something would go wrong to affect the business, even if it hurt her, she'd tell me — great loyalty. She had the last of her children while she was working here, and I wanted to be sure she stayed with me.

She's a great lady. Marvelous with my kids. Dear friends, all of them. She started with the title of secretary but she's been a lot, lot more than that. In fact, sometimes I think that — instead of the other way around — I work for her!

◆

What does wealth do to a person?

First, it makes them eat a little better and a little oftener. Other than that they have the same hang-ups everybody else does.

Wealth doesn't help anything. If you don't know how to use wealth it can be a curse and destroy you as a good human being.

Wealth gives you the opportunity to help others. It also gives you the opportunity to throw money away and pretty soon you have no wealth and then nobody wins, but first it gives you the opportunity after careful understanding to help others. That's the only thing that makes wealth a pleasure.

When you have everything you want, no matter how hard you worked for it, you still should share it with someone. Not foolishly and not letting them take advantage of you. But if they're willing to work for it, you can help them get a job, open some doors and give them a way to go, be helpful.

◆

There are no prominent people, there are just people. Prominent people may be wealthy people but they put their pants on one leg at a time just like you and I do.

You better think of your fellow man if you're going to be happy. And I think an awful lot of wealthy people do. They're always helping someone. I know of several trust funds that help a lot of kids finish school. If they're handled right, they'll be there forever.

You should be helpful and that doesn't mean you have to be an idiot about giving away all your money because then you spoil folks and they're no good. You appreciate what you earn. You don't appreciate it when it's given to you. When you're so down and low, somebody, somebody has to help you.

The difference between most people is opportunity. Opportunity has a lot to do with success.

I think of people stealing. I can understand somebody that needs bread, groceries, stealing to feed their children. But I will never understand people stealing who already have money and food to eat. There's quite a sociological difference.

People should not look at wealthy people and put them on a pedestal. They're not to be put on pedestals. But there's nothing wrong with being wealthy. Somebody earned it, either the person who has it or their family. As long as it's honestly raised and honestly earned, there's no reason to be embarrassed by it.

If you took all the wealth in the world and you split it up in the United States and you gave an equal amount to everybody in the whole country, in four or five years it would all be back in the same places.

Money is just a means to get the things you want to take care of yourself and your children.

◆

The thing that pleases me most that I've ever done is I gave the YMCA a camp for children. It's fifty miles north of here. It's in a bowl, a canyon. Has a stream through it. It has a lake. It has a forest. It's about 3,000 acres. My children were raised there. Beautiful country. It's thirty miles from Prescott. It's halfway to Flagstaff. It's the center of the state. Gave it to the YMCA with one proviso, that it must be used for families and children and if they ever do anything different, it reverts back, they lose it. So they can't sell it. It's a gorgeous place. Mountains about it. Literally thousands of people go up there every year. I gave it to them about ten years ago. It's a lovely place. That's the most satisfying thing I've ever done.

It's the Tom Chauncey H Lazy A ranch. I built it so that my own kids could be raised there and then I see these kids on the street, no place to go, no money. They need a place like that. If more children could get into a rural atmosphere and have a horse and a pig and a cow, like my children did, that would be good. So that's why I gave it to the YMCA. They've done a good job with it.

◆

The worst thing that ever happened to the city was when they stopped washing the streets. Phoenix used to be very clean. The city has a responsibility and that's to keep the streets clean. Anytime you see a picture of any major city, there's papers and dirt. That ought to be cleaned every night. We don't do enough of it.

204

And I think we need the presence of more officers on patrol. Crime is rampant and it comes with our having a good climate.

But I think they need to clean the city up like it used to be. It used to be a very clean city. They've got an awful lot of people locked up that they could take out every day with proper supervision and pick up these streets. They could take a hose and wash the streets down. They just don't seem to do it any more and I think it's too bad.

When I was in business downtown, the first thing we did every morning was clean the sidewalks. At least they had a clean place to walk down the street. We'd pick up the papers. I think it's important. I think that the dirt may be why stores moved out of downtown. Maybe they're not aware of it.

◆

There's no one man, or one person, or one group of individuals who can tell you what we're doing is right or wrong. Life goes on and we live it each day at a time. If we guess right about 50 percent of the time, we'll be fine. But we're not a perfect society.

◆

So many people come to me and they say, how do you make money? How do you become successful? What do you do, I just want to meet you. Well, that's silly. It makes me feel embarrassed. Basically what you do is you make money by saving part of what you have.

Anybody who thinks they're going to have an easy way to get money is crazy. There is no easy way. Whenever somebody says, I'll give you 15-20 per cent interest, you better keep your money in your pocket because you know there's something wrong. There's nothing in the world that can't be made a little cheaper and sold for a little less. And anybody who falls to that deserves what he gets. You can make anything cheaper, and you can sell it for a little less.

It's hard to con an honest man. A little larceny in your heart, you think you're going to make a lot of money. I think the punishment fits the greed.

205

What's the most I ever was worth? I have no idea. I never thought of it. I was talking to somebody one day about rich people or something and he said, what are you talking about? You're rich. And I said, I am? I never thought of it. And I don't think of it and I don't think most people do. You know, it's a gradual thing if you are. You're no different than anybody else. If you make ten dollars and you save two dollars or three dollars of it along the way, you can do as well as anybody.

◆

The growth of Arizona and this valley so far exceeded all of our expectations. We believed it was a good place to live. And we still think it's a good place to live. But who in the world ever believed it would develop as much as it has? Since I was a child here, people would say to me, what are all these people going to do that are coming here? Where are they going to get jobs?

Well, they're still coming here and they are working. They seem to create jobs virtually by the fact that they're here. We've become a service-oriented state. I think it's only begun to grow. The Rio Salado project could have made a world of difference. The biggest difference, nobody talked about. It would have solidified the north and south portions of this city. It would have stopped that barrier, would have let the city grow together and clean up.

◆

If the state does nothing else in my lifetime, they ought to move the damn railroad out of the heart of Phoenix. Move it out there someplace. It doesn't have to come to Phoenix, it's too close and it destroys everything around it. They won't keep it clean. They never have kept it clean. If the railroads were responsible, they'd have kept it clean. There's nothing decent going to be around it because there's not an incentive.

When I was a kid, the railroad turned off at south of Chandler. Now that it comes right into Phoenix, do you realize what it's costing us for these tracks and these things because of the railroad crossings? Why not take it out, take it the other way? And then insist that they keep it clean. They could go along those tracks with a vacuum and keep those places clean. They don't have to be a pigpen. They're destroying the heart of Phoenix and they're costing a fortune to build freeways. Take that damn railroad right-of-way and put a road in it and clean it up. It's so simple, but nobody wants to do it.

The railroads don't have the clout they used to have. They're delivering freight and they're putting the trailers on piggyback and they can haul them from out somewhere as easy as they can downtown. They don't have to destroy the heart of Phoenix. They're never going to clean it up. We've got that damn thing downtown, now let's do something.

These are the kinds of things that need to be done if you're going to stop dividing Phoenix. This is the barrier that makes South Phoenix. And South Phoenix is the worst thing that ever happened to Arizona. It should be Phoenix. It is Phoenix. It's not South Phoenix. It's only south because they thought so. They're lovely people.

I'm not anti-railroad. We have to have railroads. But they don't need them in the heart of Phoenix to separate us.

Moving them would hurt no one. You'll have people say oh, you're going to move our warehouses. Of course. And at the same time they'll tear up a lot of slums.

It's terrible what they're doing. They're getting away with murder. The railroad and the river are filthy and they've let it stay filthy. You clean up those two and move the railroad away from there, keep it out in the open spaces, and force them to keep it clean, and you'll see an entirely different city down there.

What Tom Chauncey Says

◆

I go around lots of times with no shoes on because it's comfortable. I used to do that in my office. It's comfortable. When I was a kid I had to wear everybody else's shoes, you know hand-me-downs or gimmes, and they hurt like hell because they were usually too small or too something and my feet hurt. Every time I come into the house now I take my shoes off, that's the way I grew up. I bought used shoes for fifty cents when I was a kid. The trouble is, you'd like the looks of them but they didn't always fit. It was terrible.

◆

I never liked the taste of alcohol. I drank a ton of it, but I never liked it and I watched all my friends get in trouble over alcohol. A lot of them. Booze, money, go broke. Foolish things. And about twenty-five or thirty years ago I said to myself, I am not going to go that route. I just decided I didn't want it. I didn't like it in the first place. I'd have to drink two or three drinks to get up to where I could taste it.

I just cut it off square corner. Absolutely. And I must have been gone every night for years, because it was our business, you know, motion pictures, cocktail parties and all and I never took a drink. Once in a while now I'll have a drink or two but still, I don't care for it.

◆

An important member of our family is Leah Shirk. Leah's been with me twelve years as housekeeper, kid-keeper, dog-keeper, everything-keeper, and I couldn't do without her.

Of course, she had a pretty fiery start with us — actually had three fires in the kitchen her first two weeks. My wife wanted to fire her. Fortunately, Deedie was away on a trip when the last big fire damn near burnt the house down. I called on every friend I had and before Deedie got back, the whole kitchen was rebuilt and everything was back in place and she never knew that last fire ever happened.

◆

My daily routine these days is first I check on the ranches up north and see how things are going. Then I check the rental properties. We have an apartment house and probably ten or twelve places right downtown. We have two ranches between here and town. One is thirty acres and one is five acres, horse ranches rented out. And then downtown we have a whole city block, two three-quarter blocks, couple of one-half blocks, a parking lot, all right down near where we had the TV station.

I try to stay on top of things because, you know, the best fertilizer is the footprint of the boss's shoes. Ray Sheaffer, president of Greyhound, told me that years ago. I firmly believe it. Just isn't the same if the boss doesn't go around. And the people that work there like to see you. You don't have to be isolated.

◆

What did being converted to Catholicism mean to me?

Peace. Understanding. Probably getting closer to God is the most peaceful thing that ever happened to me. In most of our minds, at least in mine, that was the one thing that was missing in my life. The closeness to God.

I think religion is the single most important thing in the world, providing you don't become bigoted and decide that you're the only one who has a right to worship the way you want to and everybody else is wrong. That's what Monsignor Donohoe was so great about. He was very ecumenical. He respected the other man's religion.

I think if you please God it doesn't matter what religion it is, if you really believe it. You really believe it. Not somebody else telling you what you believe. I don't think it matters what religion you have. When they open the doors and everybody goes in, it's a different world. That's what it means to me.

Incidentally, nobody really knows about it but once I was Grand Knight of the Knights of Columbus. Even as a convert. Great religion. Great people.

◆

My Mother was Scotch/Irish and my Father was English and Irish. I have an Irish temper. I try to control it. When I was younger I think I was more temperamental. I genuinely like people and I don't like to hurt people. I don't want to. It doesn't hurt you to smile or say a kind word or be helpful. And I think that you can't be pleasing to yourself or happy with yourself unless you live that way. You can't go through life losing your temper every five minutes because pretty soon you won't have anybody to lose it to. They'll steer clear of you. I don't think I've ever been too temperamental. I really don't. I can get pretty upset with people that I think are dishonest or have been deceitful, haven't been loyal, but fortunately, that isn't most of the time.

◆

I now have a great thing that years ago, I don't know why, they gave it to me, but I'm very grateful. I received a Doctor of Humane Letters at ASU. I didn't even know it was coming. I didn't know anything about it. I got a letter one day and I thought it was an invitation from the president over there to go do something and I laid it down and didn't look at it for a week. I didn't finish it. And then it dawned on me. I went back and I looked at that and I just didn't believe it.*

◆

I don't like to travel overseas. What can I find overseas that isn't in America in abundance, outside of being insulted, disliked, chased off of a place? Who would want to go to the Soviet Union, when you really think about it? I'd love to see the art work there, but why travel in Russia? They don't like us. Why do you go someplace you're not wanted? They'd like to cut our throats.

I think it's great that the President has come a long way with Chairman Gorbachev. I think we need to keep our guard up and I don't see why we should go over there and suffer. Some uncomfortable little lousy bed and lousy food and lousy service, and that's what you get when you go there.

---

*This wasn't the first academic distinction in the family, though. That honor went to the Rev. Charles Chauncy, an immigrant from England who was second president of Harvard College, 1654-1671, and from whose six sons and two daughters, Tom Chauncey thinks, stemmed all the rest of the Chaunc(e)y family in the U.S.

They just don't like us. The Bahamas don't like us. The Virgin Islands don't like us. They're jealous of us. You can go anywhere in Phoenix in thirty minutes and have one of the finest meals in the world. Why do you want to buy a ticket and go someplace else to eat? Talk about the great food of the world. The great food of the world is right here in America. Better service. Friendlier. In an hour you can go to Las Vegas. You don't have to go to Paris. The best shows in the world are in Las Vegas. In only a few hours, anything in the world that you could want in the United States is right here. I greatly prefer America.

England may be an exception. I think if we travel at all we ought to go to friendly countries that like us. Who wants to get up in the morning and be looking at some sour puss who doesn't like you? Hell, they call that divorce.

♦

I learned to improve my grammar by listening to good broadcasts. You listen to the kind of shows they had in those days, you learned grammar. It would grate on you if you heard the wrong words. You can learn an awful lot by watching television. You can learn the wrong things, but you can learn the right things, too. You can certainly learn proper grammar.

There were books in my home, but I rarely read a book. I'll read a book when someone hands it to me and says you must read this. Books per se, I get interested once in a while, not very often. Eventually, if a book is really good it ends up on television or on tape. Of course, it's not always the same book because they take pieces of the story.

♦

In looks I guess I favor my Mother. My Father was a huge man with coarse black hair. My Mother was smaller, with fine hair. My own hair turned white before I was twenty-nine years old, I never did know why. At first, I used to put stuff on it to keep it from looking white, then I just let it go.

♦

Occasionally, not very often, I'll go to a movie, if I see something that piques my interest. But I don't go very often. I used to go all the time. And when I was in the television and radio business I either listened to radio or had the television on all the time. I was never without. I watched television most every night, two or three shows, and watched news avidly.

I like Bob Newhart. Very funny show. He's very good. And I like "Beauty and the Beast," which is a great show. Lovely story. I liked the writing and the production. It's like the little kids with the mystery stories and the mystique that's around us. Beautiful show. And I used to like "Magnum P.I.," but it went on too long and I think what happens to those shows, those guys get to be great big stars. All of a sudden they're their own director and producer and they need somebody to say, no, you're getting too cute for this. They need a real producer and a director. That's what they're there for, to keep a star from going overboard. **211**

I still will look at "Bonanza" on a Sunday afternoon and enjoy it thoroughly. It's a fun show. I used to talk to Mr. Harris of Harris Trust in Chicago, one of the world's largest. And he and I were out on horseback one time up at the Ranchero Vistadores and he was chasing Gene Autry around like a little kid wanting his autograph and talking to him and I said, Mr. Harris, I'm curious. You obviously have all the money in the world. You can go any place in the world. You've been every place in the world. You have everything you want. You're out here on a camp with us and you tell me that you watch the "Gene Autry Show" and "Gunsmoke" every week.

Yeah.

Why?

Young man, I can sit in my living room and be outdoors.

And that's the way I feel, too. I'm a television fan. I'm a radio fan. But I guess primarily I'm a news man. That's my major.

♦

There are two subjects that are very important to me that I have not mentioned. One is the Wrigley family, with which I was associated for nearly thirty years. The other is my collection of seven wonderful children. Both were big parts of of my life, but their stories will have to wait for the next book.

◆

I daydream a lot. For instance, I'm convinced that we can clean up the pollution in this country. If we can put a man on the moon, we can clean up the atmosphere. I think somebody needs to say, probably the President, in the next five years, four years, we ought to clean up the pollution 50 percent. Then the next ten years make it 100 percent pollution-free.

Also, housing for the street people. There's no excuse in this country with the open space and the funds available, the funds we give away and send all over the world, to have people sleeping outside freezing and hungry. I don't think you should continue to feed them if they're able-bodied and could work. I think that's a mistake. But there are some that aren't.

I also dream about making the world a better place. A happier place. A place not just for me but for other people. To rid this country of drugs, and the world, too. I think drugs probably are the most devastating thing, and I think liquor contributes to using them.

When I was very active in the news business, I found it amazing that we would send our camera men and our news people to talk to knowledgeable people who should know about drugs and marijuana and the evils, the dangers of it and what it does to people, and we couldn't find any scientific person that would say it was injurious. Now here twenty, thirty years later they're saying it. Pretty late.

◆

I'll be seventy-seven years old next birthday, I don't know what it feels like to be even seventy-six years old. I think I'm forty or thirty. I don't feel any different. All I ever hope and pray is that I won't be laid up and can't get up and be productive. That's all I know how to do.

When I die I just hope my children go on and enjoy life. I don't want them crying around and moping. I've had one hell of a good time. I'm still having a good time. Life has been very good to me and I hope I've contributed something. Not ever enough, but I hope I've been a good citizen.

I don't fear death and when I do go, I hope it's quick and I don't lay around and make a nuisance of myself to a lot of people waiting on me. I don't worry about it. I don't think when you get my age it's a factor. I'm in no hurry, but I don't fear it. And I do think there's a place beyond this world.

There are some things I'd like to do. I'd like to see street people out of downtown Phoenix. I think that's a horrible thing that bothers a lot of people. If it doesn't it should. That situation alone is pretty bad. We have the money and the means to do something about it. And I don't mean give to them, I mean put them to work. But you can't put sick people and mentally retarded people all in one place. There's no escape. There's too many people in one place. There are enough ministers and churches who have programs who would take on a number of people and spread them out.

Imagine a woman and a child and a man coming here, they think they have a job. But in today's economy, after a week of not finding a job, they're broke. They can't buy gasoline. They become street people. That's not their choice. It's disgraceful, that place down there, downtown Phoenix where all those street people are, west, between the Capitol and Seventh Avenue. People sleeping out in the open in the cold weather. There's St. Vincent DePaul's which feeds a lot of them and there's a blood bank. But on any morning you can go down and see people sleeping on the sidewalks right near the police station. Lying there asleep, under a bush, or under a tree. It's terrible. And in cold weather it's worse.

♦

I also want to go up to the ranch and round up some cattle and see what kind of crop we have. Try to build a better herd than John Wayne had, and that was a good one.

Meat, regardless of what people say, is a basic commodity. It's essential to livelihood. So I'd like to produce better meat at a reasonable price.

♦

How do I explain success?

213

I firmly believe I just was in the right place at the right time. And I happen to love people. I would be no place without people. Everything that I have or don't have is because of friends and relationships. A great deal of people have helped me all my life.

And how do I want to be remembered?

I've never thought about that. I don't know. I'd like people to think I cared. That would be good enough. I think if you can do that — if people say, "well, he cared" — that's very big. That's very important.